EXPLORING NEWPORT

D1365176

By Terrence Gavan

Cover courtesy of Newport County Convention and Visitors Bureau
Photographs by Edwin Booth and Terrence Gavan

Copyright © 1992 by Terrence Gavan
ISBN 0-929249-05-4

All rights reserved. This book, or parts thereof, may not be
reproduced in any form without written permission from the author.

Published by Pineapple Publications
24 Bridge Street, Newport, RI 02840
(401) 847-0859

Table of Contents

EXPLORE NEWPORT

Explore Newport! There's so much to see and do in the City-by-the-Sea. This unique city is a virtual time capsule of Americana. Newport played starring roles in two of the great eras of American history: the Colonial Period and the Industrial Revolution/Gilded Age. Much of this history and culture is still here, for you to experience.

As a curious explorer, you'll be enthralled by the preserved architecture of Newport. But you'll also be fascinated by the cast of characters who lived here. This book is meant to guide you in your quest. It's loaded with details of Newport's houses and mansions, and it's also full of anecdotes and facts about their inhabitants. The stories of the people are mixed right in with the descriptions of the buildings. Newport's cultural heritage comes alive as you explore the neighborhoods and sections of the city, and you'll be captivated when you learn about its people.

The list of Newport superlatives is endless. Even today, in my somewhat biased opinion, Newport has to be the per capita culture capital of the United States. This mini-city offers so much: major sailing events, music festivals, libraries, museums, beaches, tennis and golf tournaments, historic neighborhoods, Gilded Age mansions, Salve Regina University and the Naval War College. The restaurants, inns and shops are also special, and a guide to them is included in this book.

This book contains nine comprehensive tours, many beginning at the Gateway Center. I recommend you park, and walk from there when possible. Walking is the best way to fully appreciate Newport.

Readers are encouraged to share their Newport experiences with me, and any relevant information not included in this book would be greatly appreciated. It's impossible to adequately explore Newport in one stay, so you'll need lots of time. Keep exploring, you'll never be bored.

Terrence Gavan
Newport, Rhode Island

About the author: Terrence Gavan has written two other books about Newport: *The Barons of Newport* and *The Complete Guide to Newport*. He has also written *A Taste of Providence* and *A Taste of Boston*. He is a certified public accountant and teaches at Salve Regina University.

NEWPORT
Historical Sketch

Early Prosperity

A group of religious dissidents from the Massachusetts Bay Colony (Boston) founded Newport in 1639. The progenitors of many renowned Newport families were in this adventurous group: Coddington, Easton, Coggeshall, Brenton, Clarke and Hazard. Through the industriousness and vision of these early colonists, Newport quickly achieved economic and cultural prominence, and during the 18th century, the City by the Sea ranked equally with New York, Boston and Philadelphia.

Throughout the first half of the 1780's, the seaport flourished as an export center for shipbuilding, farming, and manufacturing of fine furniture and silverware. Newport was a leading supplier to other coastal colonies, as well as the West Indies and Europe. The port city played a key role in the illicit but profitable "triangle trade", which involved exchanging rum, molasses and slaves between New England, Africa and the West Indies. Some of Newport's most prominent merchants were engaged in the slave trade, a principal contributor to the growth of the city's affluence.

Cultural Magnet

Increased prosperity fostered the development of the arts and trades. Architecture and carpentry thrived on the need for public buildings and homes for the affluent.

Many prominent travelers visited Newport, which was a principal gateway between the old and new worlds. Some settled in the city and greatly enhanced the cultural atmosphere. George Berkeley, a powerful figure in religion and literature, spent several years in Newport before returning to England.

An atmosphere of religious tolerance promoted the immigration of many persecuted minorities. Most notable were Quakers, Jews and Baptists. The spirit of cooperation and diligence of these people contributed much to the city's economy. It also helped create a cultural center and a cosmopolitan society unrivaled in the New World.

At an early age, Newport became a tourist center. Summer visitors came from up and down the east coast and as far away as the Caribbean. Because of its strong maritime trade, Newport had a widespread reputation. The island was known for its healthful air and mild climate. Visitors from the south mixed well and had much in common with the agriculture and merchant families of Newport.

The Revolution

The affluence and wealth of Newport's merchants attracted the attention of the British government. Perhaps it was greed, envy or an exhausted treasury (the financial result of numerous wars with France and Spain), but the "Mother" country began enforcing restrictive trade and maritime tax laws.

This led to several incidents during the late 1760's, between the British Navy and colonial rebels. Colonists burned customs ships in and around Newport harbor, and riots were widespread. The city population divided between loyalists and patriots.

The low point of Newport's history was a three-year period beginning in December 1776 when a British fleet landed with a force of 6,000 troops. The tyrannical General Prescott commanded the British occupation force and made life as wretched as possible for the colonists who remained in Newport. Many prominent families, their lives in ruin, fled the city.

Eventually the British ended their occupation upon news of an approaching French force. However, before their departure, the British looted the city, burned houses and wharves, and cut down nearly all the trees. Its economic vitality and cultural spirit destroyed, a demoralized population survived the approaching winter by ripping firewood from abandoned houses.

A mild renaissance occurred during the ensuing French occupation and restored much of the lost spirit and gaiety to Newport's soul. The gallant French officers, led by General Rochambeau, won the hearts of the people. General George Washington met Rochambeau in Newport to plan the decisive battle of Yorktown.

Transition Period

After the revolution, Newport never regained its dominance as a commercial power. Continuous maritime hostilities with England made trading difficult. Newport was practically cut-off from markets in the Caribbean. Later with the advent of the railroad, the importance of maritime trade waned, and Newport's island isolation left it cut-off from any land routes.

There was little activity in Newport during the early 1800's. A Newporter, Oliver Hazard Perry, was famous in the War of 1812 for "meeting the enemy" during the Battle of Lake Erie, and his brother Matthew Perry helped open trade with Japan. The Perrys were among the roots of the rich Naval tradition found in Newport.

By the middle of the 19th century, summer visitors began to trickle back into Newport. Slowly the city regained prominence as a tourist center. Hotels and inns flourished as resorters flocked to enjoy the healthful air and mild climate. But the advent of the Civil War abruptly ended a budding summer migration of southern gentry, mostly wealthy planters.

After the war, a large and diverse group of New England intellectuals made Newport their summer retreat and renewed the city's moribund cultural heritage. Luminaries like Oliver Wendell Holmes, Henry Wadsworth Longfellow, Henry James, Julia Ward Howe, John Singer Sargent and Edgar Allen Poe (one season) summered in Newport. Even Bret Harte livened several dinner parties during the summer of 1871.

This cultural cream, along with other wealthy Boston Brahmins, built stately but tasteful "cottages", mostly on the hill near the center of the city. The area along lower Bellevue Avenue and Ochre Point was as yet only sparsely developed.

Gilded Age

The "Gilded Age" of Newport, the splendor of which the world has rarely seen, began in the second half of the 19th century. As wealthy summer colonists built permanent residences in the general area of Bellevue Avenue, Newport gradually became the Mecca for high society and a playground for the aristocratic and nouveau rich. They arrived on their own yachts or on the luxurious paddle-wheel steamships of the Fall River Line, which plied the waters daily between New York City and Newport.

Sports thrived on the abundance of leisure time available to so many. The Newport Casino hosted the world's top tennis players, who competed on its grass courts. The first United States golf championship and international polo match were held in Newport. Sailing flourished as yacht clubs grew in popularity.

The tremendous wealth created by the Industrial Revolution and left untouched by income taxes, was lavishly spent by the barons of industrial America. They chose Newport as a principal beneficiary of this profusion and engaged highly skilled European-trained architects to construct magnificent renaissance mansions. These ornate mansions, patterned after French and Italian palaces, were the ultimate in extravagance and opulence. The Vanderbilt family played a leading role as the owner of two of the most famous mansions, "The Breakers" (Cornelius) and "Marble House" (William K.). Incredibly, most mansions were occupied for only a few weeks each summer.

Around the turn of the century, the Gilded Age was at its pinnacle. The members of the Newport high society were incessantly striving to outdo each other with grander mansions and more lavish balls. This gamesmanship led to an overkill of opulency. At one ball, guests using sterling silver shovels, retrieved party favors of rubies and sapphires buried in sand on the dining room table. Mrs. William Astor, who became the *grand dame* of Newport society, established the exclusive "four hundred"—the chosen few whose place in society was guaranteed. After World War I the Gilded Age declined and then withered away at the Great Depression.

Today Newport thrives as a tourist Mecca and cultural center. The city also enjoys an ethnic diversity. Much anecdotal history of Newport is contained in the following walking tours.

THE POINT

The Point is the epitome of Colonial Newport and one of the great preserved areas of Americana. It is the oldest section of the city, extending eastward from Washington Street to Farewell Street, covering roughly the area north of Long Wharf to the Newport Bridge.

The eminent Newport Quaker family, the Eastons, originally owned most of this section. In the early 1700s, the land was split into lots and sold to merchants, craftsmen and sea captains. The Point's principal attraction was ready accessibility to the water. Colonial craftsmen and merchants of the Point were in the export business, and their products (fine furniture, clocks, silver, pewter and whale-oil candles) could be carried easily to ships waiting in the harbor. Also, the Point was a convenient location for local smugglers to clandestinely transport booty from ships anchored in the harbor to their houses, thereby circumventing the despised British customs regulations. The most famous craftsmen of the Point were the Townsends and the Goddards—two interrelated families known throughout American history for excellence in furniture. It is believed that fourteen Townsends and Goddards worked in cabinetmaking, one was even named Townsend Goddard. As you walk the Point, you'll see several of their houses.

Most of the Point section has been meticulously restored and preserved. The neighborhoods, with narrow streets lit by gas lamps, are stunning examples of 18th century colonial architecture. Following the Quaker tradition established by William Penn in Philadelphia, most of the cross (east-west) streets on the Point are named for trees—Elm, Poplar, Willow, etc. Two north-south streets are numbered Second and Third. There's also Washington Street, a beautiful waterfront street named for the first president, who visited Newport twice. Wealthy sea captains and merchants built gambrel-roofed mansions at the head of private wharves along Washington Street, then called Water Street. There once was a Fourth Street, but America's Cup Avenue, which divides the Point, has replaced it.

Several houses in this area were moved here, either from within Newport or from some other town--an amazing testimony to the skill and ingenuity of our 18th and 19th century forebearers. You'll enjoy all the wonderful colonial (with a few Victorians and Greek Revivals thrown in) masterpieces of the Point, with their gable or gambrel roofs, beautifully pedimented doorways, and cozy rooms with handsomely constructed stairways, fireplaces and paneling. Remember these houses are not replicas like you'll find elsewhere, rather they are restored originals with much of their early structures intact.

A fascinating feature of the Point are the "hidden houses"—neat little story-and-a-half structures tucked away in the interior of a block, some with hard-to-find entrances from obscure narrow paths. Look for these "hidden houses", you should be able to find at least ten, maybe more. For the purpose of this guide the Point is divided into two walking tours, each on opposite sides of America's Cup Avenue.

The Point, West

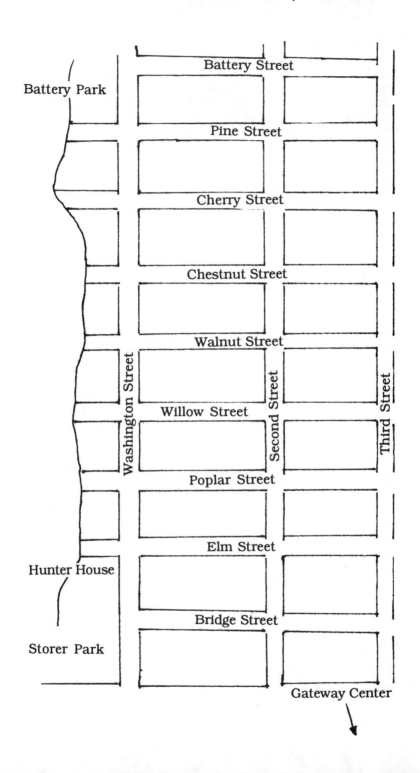

Battery Park

Battery Street

Pine Street

Cherry Street

Chestnut Street

Walnut Street

Washington Street

Second Street

Third Street

Willow Street

Poplar Street

Elm Street

Hunter House

Bridge Street

Storer Park

Gateway Center

COLONIAL NEWPORT
The Point, West

HIGHLIGHTS - On this tour you can visit Hunter House, a preserved and restored colonial mansion owned by the Preservation Society of Newport County. Also, Townsend and Goddard houses found throughout the Point are wonderful memorials to these renowned cabinetmakers. You'll marvel at the colonial architecture and the understated beauty and practicality of the area.

The western side of the Point is bordered by Newport harbor to the west and America's Cup Avenue on the east. Begin your walking tour at the Gateway Center and walk to where Washington meets the Goat Island causeway. Here you'll find **Storer Park**, a small public area offering benches, a good place to fish and a great view of the upper harbor.

The **Simeon Potter House** is across from Storer Park, at the junction of Washington Street and the Goat Island Causeway. Simeon Potter was a colonial privateer, a nice way of saying pirate. During the British war against Spain and France, privateers had *carte blanche* to attack and loot ships belonging to the enemy. Potter's pirating adventures included a raid on the South American colony of French Guiana. He led a pirate force of British men in the pillaging of a town and its church.

After the war, Potter went on to become a wealthy Bristol maritime trader. In 1772, he joined a group of Bristol friends and participated in the burning of His Majesty's customs schooner, the *Gaspee*. In 1775, Potter successfully negotiated an end to the British siege of Bristol, only later to see his Bristol house and 31 others burned by English soldiers.

In the postwar period, Simeon Potter was a philanthropist, and he donated this house (c. 1724) for use as a school for the poor. The school (Newport's first free schoolhouse) operated for about twenty years in the early 1800s. In 1882, a new school built on Elm Street was named for him. The building, now converted to residential use, still shows the pirate's name.

The **Ann Webber House** is at 33 Washington Street. This Federal style house was built in 1794 and sold in the same year for 300 silver dollars. It has a central hall, double chimneys and a fanlight doorway.

The **Isaac Dayton House** is next door at number 35. This tiny half-house with narrow windows was built around 1725. Dayton, a cordwainer, lived here prior to 1769. The left-side chimney extends from large finely panelled fireplaces. Dayton eventually went west and founded Dayton, Ohio.

At 39 Washington Street, you'll find the **Brenton Counting-House**. Built around 1748, the house was once located on Champlin's Wharf at the corner of Thames and Mary streets. It served as the accounting and administrative center for Jahleel Brenton's extensive commercial

Hunter House

Thomas Robinson House

Dennis House

enterprises. Each floor had one large room, a fireplace at one end and a stairway at the other. The gambrel roofed addition was added later.

The **Minturn House**, c.1750, is at 41 Washington Street (across Bridge Street). This gambrel roofed house once belonged to Abraham Rivera, a prominent colonial merchant. At **47 Washington Street**, there's a picturesque three-story Victorian with a steep mansard roof, high dentilled windows, (some with romantic balconies) and all sorts of fancy trim around the porch and cornices.

Walk north, and you'll soon come upon **Hunter House**, c. 1748, on the water side of the street (54 Washington Street). Hunter House, a National Historic Landmark, has been meticulously restored and is considered to be one of the finest examples of Colonial American homes.

Hunter House sits in a dominant position overlooking the harbor and was a prominent center of commercial maritime activity. The important owners of this house, although engaged in merchant activity, were well known colonial and early-American politicians.

Jonathan Nichols, a wealthy merchant and slave owner who went on to become deputy governor of the Rhode Island colony was the house's first owner. Nichols died in 1756, and soon the house along with its wharf, warehouses and outbuildings was sold to Colonel Joseph Wanton, Jr., another wealthy merchant who was also a deputy governor of Rhode Island (1764). Wanton's firm engaged in privateering and did a brisk business in the triangle trade. During this time the house and property bustled with commercial activity. Wanton was an ardent loyalist, and his steadfast support of England during the War of Independence resulted in confiscation of Hunter House by the State of Rhode Island.

In 1780, Admiral de Ternay, Commander of the French fleet used the house as his residence and headquarters. The admiral died here in December of 1780. De Ternay is buried in the Trinity churchyard. His elaborate funeral procession is said to have extended the length from this house to the church on Thames Street.

After the war, the house like the rest of Newport fell into disrepair and deterioration. In 1805, William Hunter bought the house at a sheriff's auction. In the early 1800s, Hunter was a U.S. Senator and Ambassador to Brazil.

The interior of the house, with luxurious floor-to-ceiling paneling and intricate stairway, contains priceless Townsend-Goddard furniture, Newport silver and paintings. Its pleasing and symmetrical exterior, with two enormous chimneys, is well known for the elaborate doorway, which was originally on the water side of the house. Note the pineapple in the middle above the door. There's also a beautifully restored garden in the back. Hunter House is owned by the Preservation Society of Newport County and is open to the public.

The **Elm Street Pier** is beside Hunter House. This is a perfect spot to view the Washington Street waterfront. You can sit on the wooden benches and look out to Goat Island or over to the Newport Bridge and the Naval War College.

The **Captain John Warren House** is at 62 Washington Street. This two-story gambrel roofed house, c.1736, was headquarters for the French naval artillery during the Revolutionary War. Also, the widow of artist Gilbert Stuart lived here in the early 1800s. Note the fanlight doorway.

The **Thomas Robinson House**, c. 1725, is next door at 64 Washington Street. Quaker Thomas Robinson bought this house in 1759 and furnished it with pieces supplied by neighbor John Goddard. The house served as headquarters for French Vicomte de Noailles. After the war, Mrs. Robinson corresponded regularly with the Vicomte and provided comfort following the loss of his wife and family to the guillotine during the French Revolution. Remarkably, descendants of Tom Robinson still own this house. Note the large pedimented double doorway. The house is long and deep.

The **John Dennis House**, a splendid colonial mansion, is on the corner of Washington and Popular Streets. The notorious Captain Dennis was perhaps the most successful privateer of the 18th century. From 1743 to 1756, Dennis terrorized French and Spanish shipping throughout the West Indies capturing tons of silver, gold, currency and merchandise. He even captured twenty-two free Spaniards selling them into slavery, having mistaken them for Africans. They were eventually returned after the governor of Cuba captured some of Dennis' crew. In 1756, Dennis embarked from Newport on a brand new privateering ship and was never heard from again. Dennis built this house around 1740. Note the "widow's walk" on top of the gambrel roof. Wives of sailors would look from these rooftop perches for the first sign of a returning loved one. Also note the large central chimney and intricate pineapple doorway (similar to that of Hunter House). In the late 1800s, the house was moved back from the street. The Dennis House is the rectory for nearby Saint John's church and is also used as a guest house. **Saint John's Episcopal Church** with its stone steeple is a prominent feature of the Washington Street waterfront. This "high" church offers 1928 Prayer Book services and frequent sacred music performances.

Farther north, on the water side of Washington Street, you'll find the **Sanford-Covell House** (72 Washington Street). The house was designed by Ralph Waldo Emerson's cousin and was once owned by George Bancroft, a U.S. Secretary of the Navy and founder of the Naval Academy. This Victorian-Tudor style house, built in 1870, has a large three-story, open entrance hall, stenciled ceiling, and ornately carved woods. Note the stylized mansard roof. The house is currently operated as an inn.

Sanford-Covell House

The **Finch House** at 78 Washington Street was the home of William Finch, a privateer and candle maker who boiled whale oil in the cellar. Colonial Newport was the world leader in the production of spermaceti candles. Spermaceti is a wax-like substance found in a whale's head; it burned with unusual brightness. The gambrel roofed, center-chimney house, dating from 1770, sits perpendicular to the street and has an unusual main entrance from the side.

12

Allegedly Finch built an underground tunnel from the water for the purpose of clandestinely transporting booty from privateering.

Farther along the street on the water side at **86 Washington Street** is another of the many Victorian houses on the Point. This house was built in the early 1900s by Guy and Louise Norman. The Normans were Gilded Age summer colonists who preferred Washington Street to Bellevue Avenue. Later, during World War Two, a group a Italian torpedo experts lived here. It seems the O.S.S. smuggled them out of Mussolini's Italy to Newport, where they worked to develop the magnetic torpedo exploder (Newport had a torpedo station on Goat Island). One of these men, Alfredo Sciarrotta, married and settled in Newport and went on to become a distinguished silversmith. The stucco facade masks the original wood siding of this rambling multi-gabled house, and a spacious porch offers a great water view.

Tripp House

The **John Tripp House** is next door. Originally a two-room, one-story, gambrel roofed cottage, the house was built in 1725 in Providence but moved here in 1965. The "stone-ender" chimney has a fascinating beehive oven appearing in the wall.

Continue along Washington Street, and just past Cherry Street you'll see **Stella Maris**, a 19th-century Victorian mansion now operated as an inn.

Take a break and stop at **Battery Park** (corner of Washington and Pine streets). The park is a great place to picnic and view the harbor scenery. The Newport Bridge and Rose Island provide a dramatic backdrop. As you look out, you can also see Goat Island on the left and the Naval War College on the right.

In revolutionary days, this area was a fortification used to harass British ships. Just before the British occupation, it was an enclosed fort with twelve guns. In 1798, the so-called north battery was named Fort Greene (Rhode Island revolutionary general) and refortified. In 1814, during the war with England, the Newport Artillery Company manned the fort for about six months. The fort was eventually sold to the city for use as a public park. Some remnants of the fort, which is now buried, are still visible.

From Battery Park walk eastward on Battery Street all the way down to Third Street to the facing **Southwick House**, c.1750, (77 Third Street). This house belonged to Solomon Southwick, the colonial firebrand who edited the Newport Mercury. When the British invaded Newport, Southwick buried his press and fled the city.

Turn around and go back on Battery Street to Second Street. Turn left and you'll find the **John Goddard House**, c. 1750, at number 81. This gambrel roofed house was one of the homes of the famous Newport cabinetmakers, the Goddards. The Goddards are best known for their block-front desks with shell designs. The Goddard's could never have imagined the millions that their masterpieces have commanded in recent art auctions. This house was moved here from Washington and Willow streets in 1868.

13

Perry House

Belcher House

Solomon-Townsend House

Continue south on Second Street to Chestnut Street. On the corner at 9 Chestnut, you'll find the **George Gibbs House**, c. 1734. The house has a large gable roof and two interior chimneys. Note the Dutch door. Gibbs was a baker. Cabinetmakers Thomas and Stephen Goddard also lived here.

Walk another block southward, and you'll come to the **Perry House**, c. 1750, at 31 Walnut Street. Matthew Perry was born here in 1794. Matthew along with his brother Oliver Hazard are probably the two most famous Newporters of the early 19th century. Oliver distinguished himself during the Battle of Lake Erie in 1813, and Matthew is credited with opening Japan to western trade in 1854 (an occasion celebrated annually in Newport with the Black Ships Festival). This imposing two-story, gambrel roofed Colonial mansion has fine interior paneling and a balustraded stairway. Check out the classic doorway.

Look diagonally across the street, and you'll see the quaint **Joseph Belcher House**, c. 1740, at 36 Walnut Street. Belcher was a pewterer, and his work is highly regarded. This one-story, gambrel roofed house has a fancy "S" bolt on the chimney. Check the pineapple on the post.

The **Solomon Townsend House**, c. 1725, is across the street at 51 Second Street. Townsend, a renowned cabinetmaker, built this charming house with a floor plan of three rooms surrounding a chimney. The entrance and stairway are cleverly placed in a front corner.

Walk eastward on Walnut Street to number 30, the **Cory-Townsend House**, c.1725. Another of the famous Townsend cabinetmakers, James Townsend lived here in the early 19th century. It was originally located at the corner of Washington and Willow streets. Keep walking, and look for the **William and Joseph Wanton House**, c. 1770. Note the unusual variable sized clapboards.

Walk down Third Street, turn right on Willow Street and then left onto Second Street. At the corner of Poplar Street (number 57), you'll find the **Crandall House**, another fine Point Victorian with a steep Mansard roof, fine-toothed cornice and iron-railed balcony, c.1850. The picturesque irregular lines contrast sharply with the symmetrical architecture of the Colonial period.

Look diagonally across the street to the **John Frye House**, c.1760. The gambrel roofed part was the original section of the house, which was once a bakery. Note the high chimney. Straight across the street is the **Fowler House**, c.1756, a gable roofed half-house. The interesting half-house structure was often built with future enlargement in mind. You can easily imagine a mirror image on the right side. Check out the fanlight doorway.

Go westward on Poplar Street, and you'll come to the **Chadwick House**, c.1725, (numbers 54-56), a fascinating merger of two houses. Chadwick was a ship's carpenter.

The **William Crandall House** at 63 Poplar Street is an interesting Greek Revival. This gable roofed house with end set to the street dates to 1833. The temple front with flat pillars, molded pediment-like roof line and glass paneled doorway are classic Greek Revival features. Crandall was a shipping magnate who once owned a large part of this block and a shipyard on the Point.

Walk southward on Washington Street and turn left on **Bridge Street**. Several craftsmen and sea captains lived on Bridge street, and the east end was once named Shipwrights' Street for the abundance of ship's carpenters who lived there. Bridge Street was on the north side of a now-extinct cove which extended south to Long Wharf. Ships could pass under the Long Wharf drawbridge and into the cove.

On the left, at 77 Bridge Street you'll come upon **Pitt's Head Tavern** (c. 1724). This imposing gambrel has a fascinating history starting with its original owner, Quaker businessman/culturalist Henry Collins. British trade embargoes forced Collins into bankruptcy, and in 1765 the house was sold to Robert Lillibridge, who eventually converted it to a tavern and named it for British Prime Minister William Pitt. Both British and French troops occupied this house during the Revolution. All of this early activity occurred on Washington Square before the house was moved to its present location.

The **Christopher Townsend House** (c. 1725) is a little farther down the street at the corner with Second Street. This gable-on-hip roofed house was one of the earliest houses built by the famed family of furniture makers. Walk across Second Street and look at the **John Townsend House** and Workshop, c.1750. The workshop housed a portion of the Townsend cabinet making business. Note the leaning chimney.

The diminutive **John Pain House** (c.1725) is on the corner with Third Street. According to a sign on the wall, this building was a pewter shop under grant from King George III. The **Thomas Townsend House** (c. 1735) is at the corner of Bridge and Third streets. Next door is the quite different **William Gardner House** (c. 1795), with its carved eave cornice and recessed doorway.

At this point you can walk back to the **Gateway Center** and rest.

Pitts Head Tavern

16

COLONIAL NEWPORT
The Point, East

HIGHLIGHTS - You'll find an historical treasure trove in the Island Cemetery and Common Burial Ground.

From the Gateway Center, walk to the intersection of America's Cup Avenue and Bridge Street (this is only a block away). The tour begins here.

The **Southwick House** (c. 1750), is on the corner at 31 Bridge Street. This gable roofed house was moved here from Walnut Street. The original house on this lot was moved to 23 Bridge Street. It seems the first house became too small, so a larger house was located and moved here.

Next door at 25 Bridge Street, you'll find the **Captain Peter Simon House**, a gable-on-hip roofed house built in 1727 and later enlarged. The ornate doorway was probably added in the early 1800s. The captain's son was a principal in a celebrated romantic tragedy. It seems Peter Simon, Jr., a music teacher, married Hannah Robinson over strong objections from her Quaker father. Peter brought his bride to this house, but soon deserted her after hearing that she had been disenfranchised by her father, a wealthy Narragansett planter. Hannah became despondent and lacking her father's forgiveness, died at an early age.

The **James Gardner House** (c. 1750) is the tiny gambrel next door. This is the house moved to make room for the Southwick House at 31 Bridge Street.

Look across the street to the house with the huge "S" bolts on the side wall.

This unusual building (c. 1725) was the home of **Caleb Claggett**, a baker. He was the father-in-law of George Gibbs, another baker who lived on Chestnut Street. The extensive use of brick in a wall was rare unless accompanied by a chimney. Tie rods are attached to the "S" bolts and extend through the house lending support to the masonry.

William Claggett, Caleb's son, built his house next door. This large gable roofed house (16 Bridge Street) was also built around 1725. Willam Claggett was the mechanical genius responsible for building the renowned Claggett clocks and organs. One has been in the Sabbatarian Meeting House for more than two centuries, and it's still ticking.

Walk to the end of Bridge Street to the junction with Thames Street. The next three houses were all built off the island and moved here. The **Benjamin Howland House** (c. 1721) on the corner, was a farmhouse built in Dartmouth Massachusetts. It has large granite fireplaces and an unusual gambrel roof that's not as pitched as most in Newport. Note the sliding dormer windows. Turn right on Thames Street. The the **Wilder House**, first on the right, was originally built on a farm in Johnston, Rhode Island around 1735. In the early 1970s, the Newport Restoration Foundation disassembled the house

The Point, East

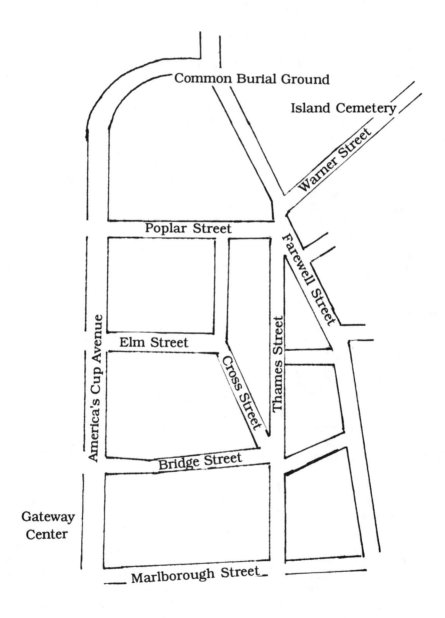

Common Burial Ground

Island Cemetery

Warner Street

Poplar Street

Farewell Street

America's Cup Avenue

Elm Street

Cross Street

Thames Street

Bridge Street

Gateway Center

Marlborough Street

Peter Simon House

Caleb Claggett House

Coddington House

and reconstructed it at this location. Next door, at 57 Thames Street, is the **Colonel Ebenezer Hathaway House**, another transplanted farmhouse. This very old gable roofed house with early hand-hewn oak construction was built in Assonet, Massachusetts around 1707.

The **Captain William Read House** is across the street at 58 Thames Street. This imposing gambrel set end to the street was built around 1740. Its fine stairway with fancy scrolls and turned balusters is thought to be made by one of the Townsend cabinetmakers.

Walk down to the corner of Thames and Marlborough streets, and on the left corner at two Marlborough Street, you'll come upon the **Governor John Coddington House**, c. 1732. The shell-hooded doorway of this elegant house is a copy of an original 1737 John Stevens carving. Around 1900, the building was raised and first floor shops opened. Later restoration returned the original design. The building houses the offices of the Newport Restoration Foundation.

Walk eastward on Marlborough Street, and you'll come to **Saint Paul's Methodist Church**. Built in 1806, Saint Paul's is the oldest Methodist church in New England. With tower in front, it's patterned after the parish churches of England. The old **Newport Jail** (now the Jail House Inn) is across the street. This brick buillding dates back to 1772.

White Horse Tavern

Keep walking to the corner of Marlborough and Farewell streets where you'll see the **White Horse Tavern**. The White horse Tavern is not a National Historic Landmark, but maybe it should be; it is the oldest operating tavern in the United States. William Mayes, a Newport pirate, established the White Horse in 1687. The sign outside says 1673, but that's when Mayes bought the building, he received a tavern license in 1687. Built around the mid 1600s, the building was originally the two-room, two-story home of Francis Brinley.

The tavern has a rich history, particularly in the 18th century. Jonathan Nichols, owner of Hunter House, operated the tavern for a time. The town council met here, and according to legend, the Rhode Island General Assembly met here before Colony House was opened in 1739. This large gambrel roofed building, one of the oldest in Newport, has an aura of the 17th century on the inside, with heavy exposed beams, a large curved-wall fireplace and central chimney.

The **Quaker Meeting House** is in the large lot across Farewell Street. Quakers of the New World were heavily persecuted and abused, particularly in Massachusetts and Connecticut, where colonists who fled religious hatred in England ironically applied this same feeling against others with different beliefs. Mary Dyer, a Newport Quaker, was expelled from Massachusetts but returned several times, at great risk, to defend her faith, she was hanged in Boston in 1660.

In 1657, hoping to find a hospitable home, the first six Quakers landed in Newport. The philosophy of this small but growing group took root among Newport's most influential families: Easton, Brenton, Coddington, Wanton and Coggeshall. Newport's Quakers went on to leading positions in government (several colonial governors) and commerce (some amassing great wealth as merchant princes). During the War of Independence, the pacifist beliefs of the Society of Friends didn't sit well with the revolutionary patriots of Newport; they destroyed Quaker houses and jailed some Quakers as traitors.

Quakers built this meeting house around 1700 (it was enlarged and altered in the 19th century), and it's believed to be the oldest one of its kind in America.

Proceed north on Farewell Street to number 33. This is the former **Quaker Schoolhouse**, built in 1711. In 1787, it was converted to a private home for Clarke Rodman, a Quaker schoolmaster.

A little farther on the left is the **Coddington Cemetery**. William Coddington, Sr., the first governor of the colony, bequeathed this land as a cemetery for Quakers. Six colonial governors--Coddingtons (two), Eastons (two), Wanton and Bull—are buried in this ancient ground. You can explore this tiny yard, and see the gravestones of Newport's prominent early families, some of which were cut at the John Stevens shop.

Continue along Farewell Street to Warner Street. The **Cozzens House** (c. 1760) is on the corner, at 57-59 Farewell Street. This huge double house consists of two separate residences. It was originally shared by two brothers, a wig maker and a hatter.

The **Almy Taggart House** is across the intersection at 56 Farewell Street. This house, c.1710, was enlarged about 1735. Note the unusual plank clapboards of different sizes.

Walk along Farewell Street, and look for the **Common Burial Ground** on the right side. This historic and hallowed ground contains over 3,000 ancient monuments with hundreds predating 1800 and some going back to the 17th century. Many early stones exhibit the carvings of William Mumford and John Stevens I and II. In a typical monument you'll see a winged head among clouds in the central arch above the inscription and foliage decorating each side. The more dense southern section of the graveyard was reserved for freemen, while the northern section was for slaves.

It's great exploring this old cemetery, it's such a poignant record of our rich heritage. Unfortunately, it's vandalized, overgrown and in general disrepair. You can walk up the hill through the Common Burial Ground and exit on the Warner Street side.

Walk a little way up the street, and you'll come to the adjacent **Island Cemetery**. These grounds are in much better condition than the Common Burial Ground, but there's still vandalism and disrepair. The Island Cemetery offers an astounding array of famous Newport and American names. The cemetery opened around 1848, and became the resting place for so many Gilded Age elite. Both Matthew and Oliver Hazard Perry are buried here. Matthew is in the Belmont section along with several other Perrys, Belmonts and Tiffanys. Oliver Hazard is in another area. The litany is extensive, some examples: Richard Morris Hunt (premier Gilded Age architect); Van Zandt, Gibbs, Griswold and Wetmore (Rhode Island governors); William Watts Sherman (Ochre Point mansion), Maude and Edith Wetmore (Chateau ser Mer); William Travers (horse owner); Janet Auchincloss (Jackie Onassis' mother); etc. In the Smith plot there's a beautiful standing angel sculpted by Augustus Saint-Gaudens (premier Gilded Age sculptor). Stop at the main house and look at the plot map, you'll find so many interesting names. The variety of stone work is fascinating.

Go back to the corner of Farewell and Warner streets. This is also the northern end of Thames Street. **William Ellery Park** is in the middle of the triangle formed by Thames and Farewell. The big tree in this park is known as the Liberty Tree. A group of zealous Newporters dedicated the original Liberty Tree in 1766 to celebrate the repeal of the despised Stamp Act, a British law requiring revenue stamps on all official documents and printed matter in the colonies. William Ellery, later a signatory of the Declaration of Independence, was part of this group.

In 1776, as the revolutionary spirit grew and animosity increased, the British ordered the Liberty Tree cut down. They could no longer tolerate the tree, which was associated with the independence movement. Earlier, a Liberty Tree in Boston met a similar fate. In 1783, another group of Newporters planted a new Liberty Tree, which remained until 1861. The current Liberty Tree, a beech, was planted in 1897. Since the revolution, Newporters have celebrated at the Liberty Tree, often by hanging lanterns on the branches. Now, on May 4th, the day Rhode Island declared independence, Newport celebrates with a parade to the tree.

Walk southward on Thames Street to the **Johnson-Braman House**, c. 1700, at number 18. This early house, set end-to-street, has a steeply-pitched gable roof and heavy exposed frames in some rooms. In 1788, the widow Johnson sold it to Mr. Braman, a caulker.

The **John Stevens Shop** is at 29 Thames Street. The Stevens were a family of master stonecutters and suppliers of gravestones. The Stevens family, particularly John I, II, and III, made most of the chimneys and fireplaces in old Newport. They also did brickwork in whaling ships and warships. And of course, they carved so many gravestones. The shop, founded in 1705, is currently run by the John Benson family, and it's believed to be the oldest continuously operated business in the United States. The houses across the street at numbers 30 and 34 were owned by members of the Stevens family.

22

Cozzens House

William Stevens and Gideon Wanton Houses

Farther along, at 44 Thames Street is the **Job Bennett House**, a gable-on-hip roofed house built around 1750. Bennett was a British loyalist who fled Newport during the Revolution.

Arnold Park is at the junction of Thames, Cross and Bridge streets. The stone marker was carved in the John Stevens Shop and represents the Newport Historic District.

Make a sharp right turn onto Cross Street and check out the **King's Arms Tavern** at 6 Cross Street. Also known as the Thomas Walker House (c. 1713), it was opened as a tavern in 1773. The Tavern was a popular watering hole for local merchants, craftsmen and politicians. Note the large overhanging cornice and huge pilastered chimney.

Continue along Cross Street, and note the **William Stevens House**, c.1720, (number 9), which has been enlarged and the tiny **Governor Gideon Wanton House** (number 11), a half-house with a steeply pitched roof and top-lighted doorway, dating to 1720.

Turn left on Elm Street. There are four noteworthy houses along this street. The **Spooner House** (1 Elm), c. 1740, is a gambrel with central chimney; the **Sherburne-Nichols House** (4 Elm), c. 1758, is gable roofed with central chimney and overhanging cornice; the **Mitchell-Trevett House** (6 Elm), c. 1785, has a nice fanlight doorway and overhanging cornice; and the **Captain Weaver House** (14 Elm), c. 1790, also has a beautiful fanlight doorway.

At this point, you should be ready to return to the Gateway Center for a rest. Turn left and walk down America's Cup Avenue.

Wanton-Lyman-Hazard House *(see page 27)*

COLONIAL NEWPORT
Historic Hill

The Historic Hill section of Newport extends east from Thames Street to Bellevue Avenue and south from Touro Street to Memorial Boulevard. Situated on a slope of a gently rising hill, this area is the most centrally located in Newport and possesses much of the charm of the original city. The highlights of this area are the colonial mansions, churches and public buildings of Newport's "Golden Age," when trade and culture flourished. In 18th-century Newport, architecture was not yet considered a profession, and buildings were designed and built by carpenters. But as construction and design became more sophisticated, these "carpenters" evolved into the equivalent of architects. Richard Munday (Trinity Church and Colony House) and Peter Harrison (Redwood Library, Brick Market and Touro Synagogue) were the two outstanding "architects" of colonial Newport. While most of the architecture is colonial, you'll also find some examples of Greek Revival, Federal Period and Victorian.

HIGHLIGHTS - There are several historically important landmarks and sites in this area. Of particular note is the Colony House, second oldest capitol building in the United States; Touro Synagogue, the first in the New World; Trinity Church, one of the earliest in the colonies; and the Brick Market, colonial center of commerce. These sites are all open for public viewing. The Wanton-Lyman-Hazard House and the Vernon House are significant examples of colonial mansions.

You can begin this tour at the Gateway Center on America's Cup Avenue. Cross America's Cup Avenue to **Cardine's Field**. This venerable ballpark was built in 1908 (four years before Boston's Fenway Park) and is the home of one of the oldest amateur baseball leagues in the United States, the George Donnelly Sunset League (started in 1919). Many great barnstorming teams and famous players have played here. The field has been restored and is in great condition. If you have time, catch a game under the lights.

Proceed west on Marlborough Street one block, and turn right on Thames Street. **Washington Square** is one block down. Washington Square was the political and economic center of colonial Newport. In the 18th century, this area was a beehive of activity with the Colony House (center of government) on one end and the Brick Market (center of commerce) on the other.

At the foot of the square is the **Brick Market**, a National Historic Landmark built in 1772. This open-air market house was designed by Peter Harrison and represents a unique architectural style for Newport. Numerous archways on the ground floor are particularly representative of the Palladian architectural style that was popular in 18th century England. Pedimented windows between large ionic

25

Historic Hill

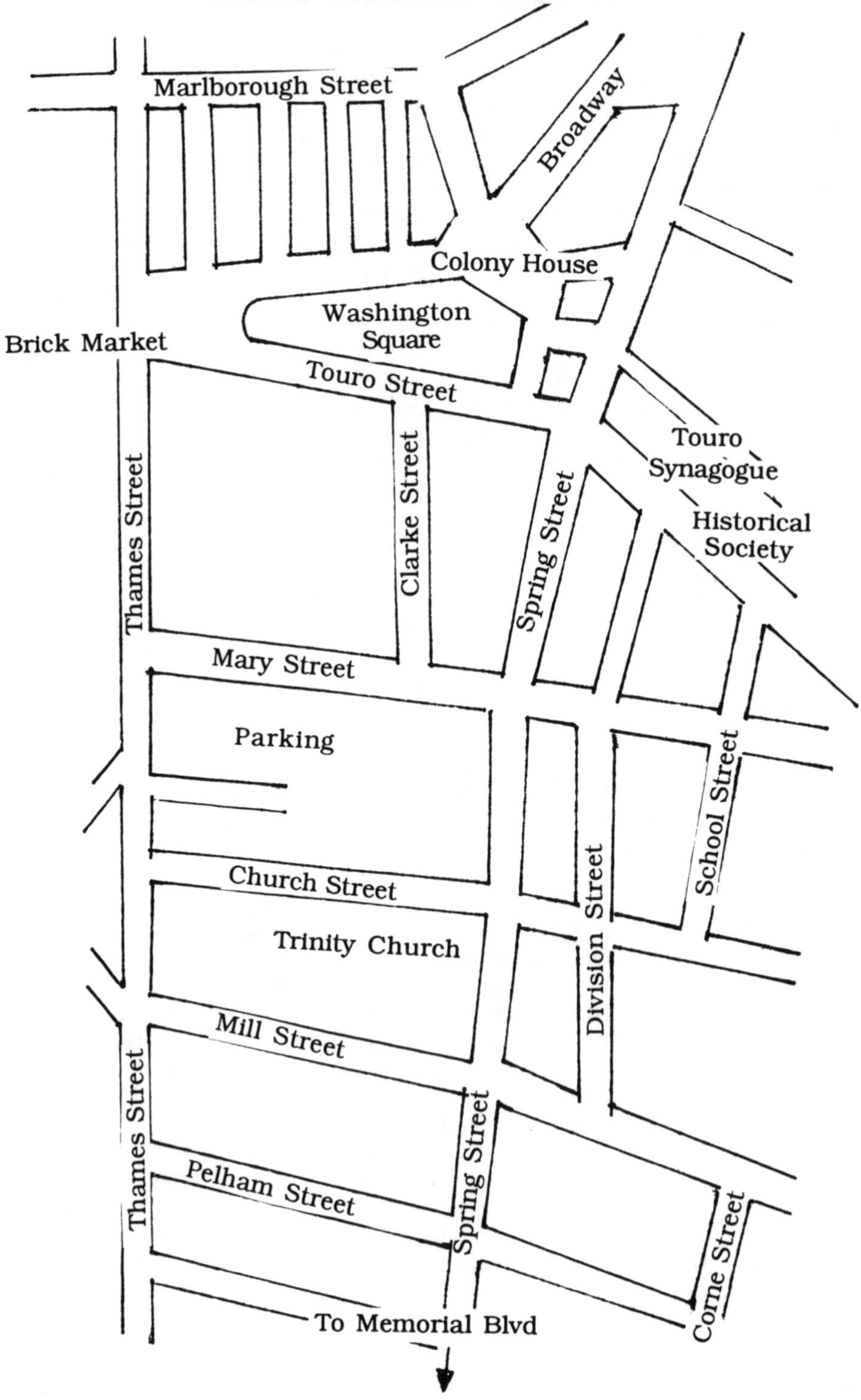

Marlborough Street

Broadway

Colony House

Washington Square

Brick Market

Touro Street

Thames Street

Clarke Street

Spring Street

Touro Synagogue

Historical Society

Mary Street

Parking

School Street

Church Street

Trinity Church

Division Street

Mill Street

Thames Street

Spring Street

Pelham Street

Corne Street

To Memorial Blvd

columns (pilasters) dominate the classic facade on the upper floors. In the 18th century, the arcade on the ground floor teemed with merchants and traders and was testimony to the commercial importance of colonial Newport. In 1842, the arches were closed, and the building was converted to the town hall. Now, the Brick Market is restored to its former elegance and is open to the public as a museum of Newport's heritage.

Eisenhower Park is in the middle of Washington Square. Here you can relax and absorb the panorama of old Newport. Note the statue of Newporter Oliver Hazard Perry.

While you're here, take a look at the other notable buildings in the Square. The **Rivera House** is at the foot of the Square near the Brick Market. This large gambrel was the home of Abraham Rivera, a prominent Jewish merchant who started the lucrative sperm oil industry in the colonies. Rivera was also a highly regarded cultural leader. He helped build Touro Synagogue and helped start the Redwood Library. Citizen's Bank now occupies this building.

The **Peter Buliod House**, c. 1750, is across the Square at 29 Touro Street. This large house has a shallow hip roof, ornate cornices, classic Greek Revival doorway and a wood block facade that simulates stone. The stairway and rich interior paneling are from the demolished Jahleel Brenton Mansion. Oliver Hazard Perry lived here for a short time in 1818.

The **Joseph and Robert Rogers House** is next door at 33 Touro Street. This handsome three-story hip roofed mansion was built around 1798. The house exhibits features of the Federal period with its Corinthian columned doorway.

The **Wilbour-Ellery House**, farther up the street, is another large hip roofed mansion built about 1801. The interior exhibits Federal period woodwork with fine mantles and archways. Note the similarity to the doorway of the Rogers House. In 1809, William Ellery III, whose father signed the Declaration of Independence, lived here.

Colony House, built in 1739, is at the head of the square but to the left of the Newport County Courthouse as you look up. Until the new Providence state house opened in 1900, Colony House was the principal seat of government for the Colony and State of Rhode Island. Richard Munday designed Colony House patterning its pleasing symmetrical exterior after 17th century English manor houses.

From the central balcony the coronation of King George was announced in 1760, as was the repeal of the Stamp Act in 1766 and the Declaration of Independence in 1776. Both the British and French armies occupied Colony House during their stay in Newport. George Washington visited Colony House twice: in 1781, to meet with French General Rochambeau; and in 1790 for a festive victory celebration. Washington's portrait, by Rhode Island artist Gilbert Stuart, hangs upstairs. Colony House is a National Historic Landmark and is open to the public.

Walk past Colony House, a short distance up Broadway, and you'll come to the **Wanton-Lyman-Hazard House**. The house is located on the right side of the street at 17 Broadway. Built around 1675, this

Buliod House

Colony House

National Historic Landmark is the oldest private residence in Newport. The stamp master of Newport (charged with enforcing the hated Stamp Act) owned this house until he was run out of town in 1765 by an angry mob during the Stamp Act riot. Not the most popular man, Martin Howard, a staunch loyalist, barely made it to a British ship anchored in the harbor before the mob ransacked his house, ripping down the lovely paneling and smashing windows. Howard never returned.

John Wanton, of the renowned Quaker family, bought the house in 1772. During the French occupation, his daughter Polly enchanted Rochambeau's officers and supposedly moved one to etch "Charming Polly Wanton" on a window pane. Polly was one of the "belles" of Newport, and the house was a center of merriment during this brief renaissance. Polly later married Daniel Lyman, and the house eventually passed to their son-in-law, Benjamin Hazard.

Although built in the 1600s, The house was renovated in the 1700s and displays architectural elements from both centuries. Of particular interest is the winding stairway, massive exposed beams and corner posts, and the fine detail on the chimney. You can see the inside of this house because it's owned by the Newport Historical Society and open to the public.

Touro Synagogue

Walk up to Spring Street via Stone Street, the short cross street on the corner at Broadway. Turn right and go down a short distance to Touro Street, then turn left and walk up the hill to **Touro Synagogue**. The oldest synagogue in the United States, Touro Synagogue is a National Historic Site. Newport's Jewish community started in 1658 when fifteen families arrived from Holland. Through the century the congregation increased steadily with families coming from Portugal and Curacao.

Jews numbered among the prominent merchants and community leaders of colonial Newport. Unfortunately, Jews remained second-class citizens and were not allowed to vote until the revolution. For 100 years the Jeshuat Israel worshipped in private homes until Rabbi Isaac De Touro encouraged the construction of this classic synagogue. In 1763, Touro Synagogue opened for worship containing the Torah that accompanied the first Jews to Newport. George Washington wrote the congregation in 1790, expressing the ideal that the newborn country would give "bigotry no sanction and persecution no assistance."

The exterior has a simple but classic style exemplified in the columned portico over the entrance. Upon entering, you'll don a yarmulke and behold an exquisite interior. Peter Harrison designed Touro Synagogue, and it is believed that Secretary of State Thomas Jefferson, accompanying President Washington to Newport (in 1790), was so enamored of Harrison's design that it inspired the planning for his own Monticello. Touro Synagogue is monumental testimony to the spirit of religious tolerance that so dominated colonial Newport.

The **Newport Historical Society** is next door at 82 Touro Street. This is also the site of the **Sabbatarian Meeting House** (attached at the back of the building). The meeting house (c. 1729), which was moved here, was the home of the first congregation of Seventh Day Baptists, formed in 1671 by Stephen Mumford. The house contains a clock made by William Claggett. If you're interested in Newport history, browse through the Society's well-stocked library, and also check out the collection of Newport furniture and other exhibits.

Go back down Touro Street, and look for the **Levi Gale House** across from Touro Synagogue. This Greek Revival house was designed by Russell Warren and built around 1835. Note the huge fluted pilasters and the columned portico. Before 1915, the house stood at the head of Washington Square, the present site of the county courthouse.

You're now at the corner of Touro and Division streets. Walk down Division Street, and you'll see several notable houses of the Colonial period, mostly small gable-roofed houses some with wide overhanging cornices. Continue across Mary Street to the **Lucas-Johnston House** (c. 1721) at 40 Division Street. Augustus Lucas was a French merchant who came to Newport in the early 18th century and began selling slaves. At one time the house was rented to Robert Gardner who performed pear grafting experiments in the garden. Lucas' grandson, Augustus Johnston was a prominent colonial leader as Attorney General of the colony and Stamp Master. Johnston Rhode Island is named after him. He eventually fled Newport for the south. Later French soldiers occupied the house. Also, Oliver Hazard Perry lived in this house in 1813-14.

The **Reverend Samuel Hopkins House** is at 46 Division Street. This end-to-the-street gambrel was built around 1751. Doctor Hopkins, a staunch abolitionist and pastor of the First Congregational Church, lived here in the late 18th century and was the hero of Harriet Beecher Stowe's novel, The Minister's Wooing.

CORNE HOUSE
Home of the artist
MICHEL FELICE CORNE
who introduced the tomato
into this country

Turn left, and take a short walk up Church Street to number 78. This is the **Thomas Goddard House**, c. 1800, it belonged to another of those renowned furniture makers.

Go back down to Division Street, turn left, walk to the end, and then turn left again at Mill Street. Go up the hill to Corne Street, and at the corner you'll find the former home (c. 1800) of **Michel Felice Corne**, the famous Italian muralist. Corne was well-known for seascapes and Great Lake battle scenes. He is also credited with introducing the tomato to the colonies.

Continue along Corne Street to Pelham Street, and at 92 Pelham you'll see the **Butler House**, an elaborate Victorian house built in balloon-framing around 1865. Note the different kinds of trim and the Victorian tower.

Turn right, and go down Pelham Street to the **Arnold Burying Ground**. Governor Benedict Arnold and much of his family are buried here. Arnold was the first governor of the Colony of Rhode Island (and grandfather of the infamous traitor). His family owned most of this area. This is a fascinating little cemetery containing many gravestones (most in good condition) from the late 17th and early 18th centuries. Note the stone in front of the fence dated 1795 and signed by John Stevens.

The **Augustus Littlefield House** is an exemplary Greek Revival at 70 Pelham Street, next to the cemetery. Captain Littlefield built this house in 1836, patterning it after Italian villas seen on his voyages. The massive temple facade with pedimented portico dominates the front. Rhode Island governor Charles Van Zandt lived here from 1863 to 1890.

Continue down Pelham Street to Spring Street. The **John Bannister House** (56 Pelham Street) is at the corner. Bannister, a merchant prince and smuggler, built this large gambrel in 1751. General Richard Prescott, commander of the British occupation force, made this house his headquarters. Prescott had no use for Newporters and the feeling was mutual during his reign of humiliation and destruction.

Look across the street at the majestic **Newport Congregational Church**, built in 1857 in the Roman Revival style. Master decorator John La Farge made the stained-glass windows and decorated the interior with murals.

Walk south (turn left) on Spring Street to John Street. The **Bull-Mawdsley House** is on the left at 228 Spring Street. In 1680, Governor Benedict Arnold's son-in-law, Jireh Bull, built part (four rooms) of this house. In 1750, Captain John Mawdsley, a wealthy merchant, built two more rooms and the facade. This house served as the headquarters for the second-in-command of the French army, the Marquis de Chastellux.

Continue along Spring Street to Memorial Boulevard, turn right and follow Memorial Boulevard down the hill to the Post Office. Now you're at Thames Street. To the left is lower Thames, the home of wharves, shops and restaurants, and to the right is upper Thames which parallels America's Cup Avenue. Turn right, and walk up Thames Street a few blocks to **Queen Anne Square**. The square is bordered by Mill Street on the south side and Church Street on the north. Queen Anne Square is lined with exquisitely restored colonial houses. But the most prominent structure in the square is the striking **Trinity Church**. Trinity Church, with its lofty clock tower, is the most prominent landmark on Newport's waterfront skyline. The church was colonial Newport's representative of the Church of England.

Richard Munday, who built Colony House, designed this National Historic Landmark in 1726, patterning it after Boston's Old North Church. George Berkeley, one of the most influential theologians of the 18th century, preached here often during his residency in Newport. George Washington attended services at Trinity, and Admiral de Ternay, commander of the French fleet, is buried in the churchyard. After the British occupation, Newporters sacked the church, destroying all symbols of England save the bishop's mitre: it was out of reach, high on the steeple. The interior has galleries on each side, box pews, a triple decked pulpit, Tiffany stained glass and many other works of art. During the Gilded Age many of Newport's wealthy families like the Vanderbilts had private pews.

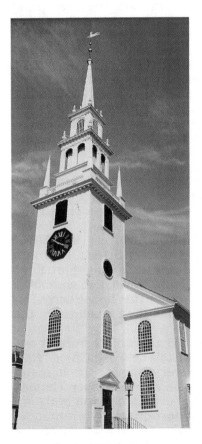

Trinity Church

While in Queen Anne Square, take a moment to relax and imbibe the colonial ambiance provided by the surrounding houses, church and churchyard. During the United States Bicentennial celebration in 1976, Queen Elizabeth II visited Newport and dedicated this square (look for the plaque in the middle).

Walk up through the graveyard at the left of the church to Spring Street, and turn left. Continue north on Spring for one block, turn left on Mary Street, and go down the hill to Clarke Street. **Vernon House** (c. 1700), a National Historic Landmark and one of the most historic houses in Newport, is on the corner. Lafayette and George Washington were guests here. Washington visited French General Rochambeau at this house in 1781 to discuss war plans. Rochambeau used this house as his headquarters while the French army occupied Newport.

Rochambeau's army, composed of the finest noblemen leading elite regiments, charmed the population, particularly the young ladies. French officers escorted the belles of Newport everywhere—to balls, teas and on walks through town--and romance flourished. Most of Newport turned out for an emotional send-off when the army sailed to eventual victory at Yorktown.

Metcalf Bowler, a Chief Justice of the Rhode Island Supreme Court, bought this house in 1759. In 1760, he substantially reconstructed and enlarged the house, employing Peter Harrison as the architect. In an ironic twist, a recent discovery indicated that Bowler had been a British spy during the Revolution.

In 1774, Bowler sold this house to William Vernon, an avid patriot who later fled the British occupation. Vernon was a wealthy ship owner, slave trader and a founding father of the American Navy. When he bought this house just prior to the abolition of slavery in Rhode Island, Vernon possessed five household slaves. During the revolution, Vernon fled to Boston and headed the newly formed Navy board. After the war, Vernon returned to Newport and founded the Newport Bank in 1805.

The exterior of this elegant mansion looks like rusticated stone, but look closely, it's really wood. The interior has a long hallway divided by an arch and extensive paneling on the ground floor. Sometime in the early 1900s, the paneling in one room was removed to reveal Chinese paintings dating to 1730. It seems they were covered up in Metcalf Bowler's 1760 reconstruction.

Walk along Clarke Street. It's replete with classic 18th century houses, but in their midst is a 19th century armory. The building at 23 Clarke Street is the home of the **Artillery Company of Newport**. Chartered in 1741 by King George II, it is the oldest active military organization in the United States. Stonemason Alexander McGregor, builder of Perry Mill and Fort Adams, built this armory in 1836. The armory is now a museum containing a vast collection of military mementos and memorabilia. The military uniform collection is particularly notable and contains uniforms of Anwar Sadat, King Hussein, Prince Philip and Field Marshall Montgomery to name a few.

The **Second Congregational Church Meeting House** is next door. This congregation is famous for its eminent colonial pastor, Ezra Stiles. The erudite Stiles, whose education and intellectual acumen were unrivaled, was a renaissance man--writer, scientist, educator and cleric. His writings provide a valuable understanding of colonial America. When the French arrived in Newport to aid the patriot cause, he described the great joy: "The bell rang at Newport till after midnight and the evening of the 12th Newport illuminated; the Whigs put thirteen lights in the windows, the Tories or doubtfuls four or six. The Quakers did not choose their lights should shine before men, and their windows were broken."

Stiles dabbled in electricity, studied stars and silkworms, wrote history, helped start Brown University and went on to become president of Yale.

This church was built in 1735 and used as a hospital by both the British and the French. Stiles' house is across the street at **14 Clarke Street**.

Continue along Clarke Street into to Washington Square. You can walk through the square and back to the Gateway center.

Vernon House

Reading Room

Redwood Library

VICTORIAN NEWPORT
Top of the Hill

HIGHLIGHTS - The Victorian gems, which are so whimsical and wonderfully romantic, add to the cachet of Newport as an architectural gold mine. Wealthy intellectuals and artists of the late 19th century made their summer homes in this area, setting the stage for the later invasion of the *nouveau riche* of the Gilded Age. Redwood Library, a masterpiece from the colonial era, is also in this section.

Start this tour at the beginning of Bellevue Avenue where Touro and Kay streets intersect. As you look down the famed Bellevue Avenue, the stately Viking Hotel is on the right and the **Jewish Cemetery** is on the left. This graveyard contains stones dating from 1761 with inscriptions in Hebrew, Latin, Portuguese, Spanish and English. Newport's Jewish community bought this land in 1677.

Walk down the avenue to the corner with Church Street, and you'll find the venerable **Newport Reading Room**. This Greek Revival house was acquired from the William Potter estate in 1854 and established as a private club. The Reading Room was a favorite refuge for the titans of the Gilded Age. This exclusive men's organization was Newport's counterpart to New York's Knickerbocker and Century clubs and Boston's Somerset and Tavern clubs. Not a lot of Reading was done here during the Gilded Age, but there was a lot of imbibing and conviviality. It was a welcome escape from the tedious socializing of Newport's matrons. The club may have been indirectly responsible for the founding of the Newport Casino. It seems that clubman James Gordon Bennett, an early Newport resorter and publishing magnate, was in one of his frequent rowdy moods when he challenged his friend, Captain "Sugar" Candy, a British lancer and polo player to gallop his horse across the porch. Candy accepted the challenge and charged up the stairs and into the hall, routing the astonished clubmen. After a club censure, a surprised and incensed Bennett decided to start his own club and founded the Newport Casino.

In 1925, hard living alcoholic Reggie Vanderbilt went straight for the Reading Room bar after arriving from a European "drying out" trip. He promptly got drunk, and two weeks later he died of internal hemorrhaging, setting off a chain of events in the epic child custody story of his daughter Gloria Vanderbilt.

Continue along Bellevue Avenue to Redwood Street and the **Redwood Library**. It looks like an ancient temple, but the blocks are wood, not stone. Built in 1748, Redwood is the oldest continuously-used library in the United States and was the logical extension of the Literary and Philosophical Society founded by Dean George Berkeley, Henry Collins and Abraham Redwood in 1730.

This classic Roman Doric temple had profound influence on the architecture of American public buildings. Keeping with Newport

Top of the Hill

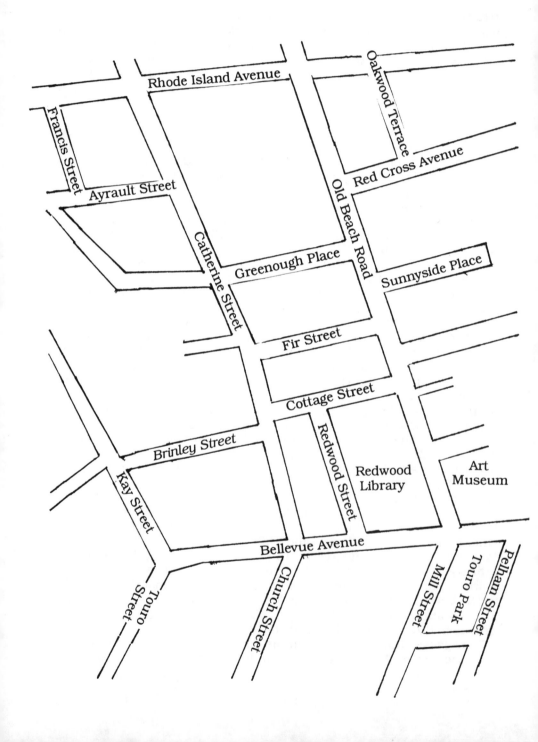

tradition the construction is wood, but the walls are rusticated and painted to simulate stone. The building has been rearranged and enlarged several times by prominent architects who kept Harrison's theme intact.

The library contains painting by several famous Newport artists: Gilbert Stuart, John Smilbert, Michel Felice Corne and Edward Bannister. It also has an ancient and ticking Claggett clock and a 1758 map of Newport by Ezra Stiles. This Peter Harrison masterpiece and National Historic Landmark helped place Newport (even ahead of New York and Boston) at the cultural center of colonial America.

Across the avenue is a delightful Victorian, the petite **Samuel Pratt House** (a.k.a. Bird's Nest Cottage), built in 1871. Located at 49 Bellevue Avenue, this picturesque stick-style house features colored slate sides, fanciful towers and all kinds of fancy trim. Pratt was a Boston architect.

Touro Park lies a short distance down Bellevue Avenue between Mill and Pelham streets. One of the highest points in Newport, Touro Park is a great place to relax and enjoy the surrounding architecture. The park is the home of the mysterious Stone Tower, which according to some, was built by Viking explorers in the 11th century. Another theory attributes the tower to early Portuguese explorers. However, colonial governor Benedict Arnold, who owned most of this land, is also believed to have built the tower, whose arches face the basic points of the compass.

Along the adjoining Mill Street are the **Charles Sherman House** (128 Mill Street), an end-to-street Greek Revival built in 1850 and the **Robert Lawton House** (118 Mill Street), a stately brick Federal style house with balconied portico and cyclopean window, built in 1809.

Art Museum

On the west side of Touro Park at **5 Touro Park West**, you'll see an elegant hip roofed mansion featuring Victorian, Federal and Greek Revival details

Several houses of interest line Pelham Street on the south side of the park. The **Swinburne House** (115 Pelham Street) is an 18th century Greek Revival with rusticated corners and ionic columns supporting the portico. The **White House** (c.1847), built by master mariner Robinson Gardner, is another classic Greek Revival at 123 Pelham Street. There are also two fine Victorians: **135 Pelham Street** (note the tower and the elaborate shingles and trim) and the **Seth Stitt House** with its spacious wrap-around verandah, at 141 Pelham Street. The latter house was built in 1877 by George Champlin Mason, and it was the location of the United States Naval Academy during the Civil War (it's now the Elks Club).

The **Channing Memorial Church**, built in 1881, is also on Pelham Street. Named for the originator of American Unitarianism, Newporter William Channing, this rough-cut granite church contains stained-glass windows by John La Farge and a bronze plaque by Augustus Saint-Gaudens. Poet Julia Ward Howe was a member of the congregation.

The **Newport Art Museum** is across Bellevue Avenue from Touro Park. This huge European-style chalet with medieval half timbering was designed by premier Gilded Age architect Richard Morris Hunt in 1862 (Hunt's first Newport commission). The skeletal stick-style design contrasts sharply with Hunt's great stone palaces of the Gilded Age and is considered his most "American" creation. This picturesque balloon-framed Victorian building abounds with gables, bays and piazzas. The high-ceilinged interior gives a free flowing impression with its octagonal central hall surrounded by polygonal rooms with wide doorways. The adjoining **Cushing Gallery** looks like an ancient temple.

Walk along Old Beach Road (the art museum is at the beginning of Old Beach Road) and you'll come upon several notable 19th century mansions. The **Commodore William Edgar House**, at 29 Old Beach Road, was built in 1886 by the renowned Gilded Age architectural firm of McKim, Mead and White. William Edgar was a longtime summer resident and was a commodore of the New York Yacht Club for many years.

This unique brick mansion has been criticized for being arbitrary and awkward in design. The size and placement of windows and the shapes of the projecting bays are varied and asymmetrical. The porch over the drawing room on one side offsets the smooth solid brick of the service wing on the other side. The walls are made of buff Roman brick, and the roof is slate shingled. The rooms are finished in oak, pine and cherry. The cost of the house was $42,870.

Walk down Sunnyside Place which borders the Commodore Edgar property. The building on the corner is the **George Champlin Mason House** at 31 Old Beach Road. Mason, an architect and author, combined English half timbering and Swiss chalet gables into his 1874 home. Note the elaborate ornamental trim and broad projecting eaves. The house was known as the Woodbine Cottage.

38

Commodore Edgar House

Colman House

Mason designed the house at **6 Sunnyside Place** for Edward Brinley in 1873. Famed Gilded Age painter and stained-glass artist John La Farge summered in the Greek Revival house at **10 Sunnyside Place** (c.1845).

Tilton-Hobbs House

The **Tilton-Hobbs House** is at the end of the street. McKim, Mead and White designed this house in 1882. It has all sorts of interesting exterior features: stone base, chips of colored glass embedded in plaster, fancy shingles, a profusion of little windows an elaborate chimney. Tilton was a milliner with stores in Boston and Paris.

Go back to Old Beach Road, turn right, and continue along Old Beach Road to Red Cross Avenue. The **Belair Mansion** (c. 1850) is at 34 Old Beach Road opposite Red Cross Avenue.

This imposing stone Italianate villa with its block tower and mansard roof was owned by George Norman, a civil engineer who founded the Newport Water Works.

Go down Red Cross Avenue, and you'll see three more McKim, Mead and White houses in this area. The **Catherine Prescott Wormeley House**, a large multi-gabled Queen Anne built in 1877, is on the corner at 2 Red Cross Avenue. Note the three-story tower topped by an onion dome. Wormeley was a Civil War diarist and author.

The shingle-style **Skinner House** (a.k.a. Villino), c. 1882, at 6 Red Cross Avenue (on the left after number 4) is a good example of open planning in a relatively small house. The rooms are arranged around a pivotal hall and fireplace and connected by several doorways. Note the roundhouse tower and fancy chimney.

The **Samuel Colman House** (a.k.a. Whileaway), built in 1883, is across the street and farther down (past Oakwood Terrace), at 7 Red Cross Avenue. Colman was a wealthy landscape artist, interior decorator and first president of the American Watercolor Society. He decorated the rooms with all sorts of Japanese objects of art. The shingle-style house with its gambrel roof looks a bit like a converted barn. Note the enclosed loggias, enormous chimneys, expansive stone terrace and the rough stone base. The house was built for about $25,000.

Double back to Oakwood Terrace, and you'll find **Oakwood**, a three-story 19th century Colonial Revival mansion, at the corner. Note the pebbled surface and the Corinthian columned doorway.

Walk east on Oakwood Terrace one block to Rhode Island Avenue, turn left and walk toward Old Beach Road. This section of Rhode Island Avenue was called Lovers Lane because of its tree-lined seclusion. Be careful, there's no sidewalk here. Continue along Rhode Island Avenue past Catherine Street to Francis Street. Turn left on

40

Francis Street and work your way back to Bellevue Avenue. This general area is truly **Victorian Newport**. As you walk this area, note the spectacular variety of 19th century mansions. You'll find great stone castles; romantic Victorian mansions with towers, turrets and gables abounding; as well as a mixture Tudors, Queen Annes and Greek Revivals.

Another McKim, Mead and White house is at the corner of Rhode Island Avenue and Francis Street (**15 Francis Street**). This large multi-gabled, multi-chimneyed house displays a profusion of shingles. Large gables are set at right angles, one even has a gambrel shape. Windows of different sizes are placed throughout the shingled exterior.

The **Mary Mitchell House** (c. 1880) is next door on Francis Street. George Champlin Mason designed this large clapboard house, with its expansive porch and fine trim. Note the many gables symmetrically arranged and varied in size. **11 Francis Street** is another McKim, Mead and White house, with a clapboard and shingle exterior and broad gables.

Walk westward on Francis Street to Ayrault Street, turn left and continue along to Catherine Street. Turn right on Catherine, and head toward Bellevue Avenue.

The cottage at the corner of Greenough Place and Catherine Street (33 Catherine Street) is the **Colonel George Waring House** (a.k.a. The Hypotenuse). Richard Morris Hunt built this house for himself in 1871 and later sold it to Colonel Waring. This quaint cottage shows some Colonial Revival (a style that hadn't really started yet) influence with its symmetrical lines. The eclectic design features Greek columns in the recessed doorway, a gambrel and hip roof and an odd center gable with perforated Swiss chalet style trim. Hunt moved the house here from its original site at the beginning of Bellevue Avenue, the current location of the Viking Hotel.

Continue west on Catherine Street, and you'll find the **Clement C. Moore House** (c. 1850) at 35 Catherine Street. Professor Moore was a respected scholar of oriental and Greek literature, but he is best known as the author of "The Night Before Christmas". He summered here for several years. Note the expansive porch and the Victorian tower. This house was also known as Tudor Hall.

Farther along at 20 Catherine Street, you'll find the **King-Birkhead House**, c.1872. Dudley Newton designed this mansard roofed house for Dr. David King and his son-in-law Dr. William Birkhead. Note the high tower and the dormers projecting below the roofline.

You can continue along Catherine Street back to Bellevue Avenue, near the Viking Hotel. However, there are several more streets in this general area (called the "Top of the Hill") which you may wish to explore, particularly the area along and around Kay Street.

Newport Casino

Kingscote

Berkeley Villa

GILDED NEWPORT
Bellevue Avenue

HIGHLIGHTS - Bellevue Avenue itself is a highlight of this tour. This elegant avenue will remain an important part of Americana, on a par with Fifth Avenue, Worth Avenue, Beacon Street and Wall Street. This is mansion country, and many are open for public touring: The Elms, Chateau-sur-Mer, Rosecliff, Beechwood, Marble House and Belcourt Castle.

The tour starts at the intersection of Bellevue Avenue and Memorial Boulevard and covers most of the "Avenue", all the way down to Bailey's Beach. Bellevue Avenue is restored to much of its former splendor with a spotless concrete surface, brick and gravel sidewalks and old fashion gaslights. The broad street is a stunning sight in the evening, lit by soft gaslight and lined with ancient trees and magnificent mansions.

The **Travers Block** is on the left side as you face south from the corner of Bellevue Avenue and Memorial Boulevard. In 1875, Richard Morris Hunt designed this medieval row of half-timbered retail shops and bachelor apartments (now offices). The building is named for horseman William Travers (the Travers Stakes) who lost the property while gambling at the nearby Canfield House.

The famed **Newport Casino** (c.1880) is next door. This august institution was America's first country club and hosted the first national tennis championship in 1881. The tournament remained at the casino until 1915, when it moved to Forest Hills, New York (it now resides at Flushing Meadows, New York). As the birthplace of American lawn tennis, the casino houses the International Tennis Hall of Fame, a museum with exhibits of art, trophies and other memorabilia. Since 1955, the legends of tennis have been enshrined annually in the Hall of Fame. In addition to the museum, the complex contains the 19th century Horseshoe Piazza with a lush tennis and croquet court, a main grass court stadium, several manicured grass courts, an indoor theatre and a restored royal tennis court portraying the ancient sport as it was played in 13th century Europe. The casino now hosts the only grass court professional men's and women's tournaments in the United States.

The Newport Casino was the brainchild of James Gordon Bennett, Jr., an overbearing iconoclast who was a publishing and yachting pioneer. Bennett was truly a driven man and created the casino out of spite for the Newport establishment, when the venerable Reading room censured him (see Victorian tour).

Bennett was the publisher of the New York Herald and the Paris Herald, and he was also famous for sending Stanley into Africa to find Livingstone. He was a yachtsman extraordinaire, and was commodore of the New York Yacht Club. Bennett was a flamboyant big spender

Bellevue Avenue

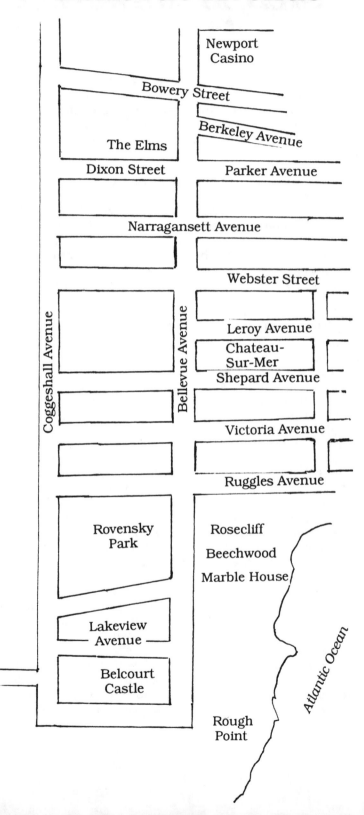

Newport Casino

Bowery Street

Berkeley Avenue

The Elms

Dixon Street

Parker Avenue

Narragansett Avenue

Webster Street

Coggeshall Avenue

Bellevue Avenue

Leroy Avenue

Chateau-
Sur-Mer

Shepard Avenue

Victoria Avenue

Ruggles Avenue

Rovensky
Park

Rosecliff

Beechwood

Marble House

Lakeview
Avenue

Atlantic Ocean

Belcourt
Castle

Rough
Point

who easily went through thirty million dollars on his various whimsical projects.

After the Reading Room censure, Bennett thumbed his nose at established Newport and hired renowned architect Stanford White to build this modern country club to be used for tennis, concerts, card playing and dancing.

The clubhouse combines Victorian charm with Chinese detail. Its shingled exterior and multi-gabled roof line surrounds a picturesque courtyard with a clock tower, horseshoe piazza and several latticed porches.

Each Gilded Age summer morning, club members would gossip from the second floor terrace while a string orchestra played on the piazza. In those days, only bluebloods played in tennis tournaments, and Boston Brahmin Richard Sears, decked in knickers, with wool socks, blazer, cap and rubber-soled canvas shoes, won the championship eight years in a row.

Tennis Week was a social highlight every August, as Newport's elite displayed themselves to each other in the highest of fashion. Grandstand seats were status symbols granted by birthright to the cream of American society. Of course every year the same seats went to the Vanderbilts, Astors, Belmonts and Goelets.

The casino became the cultural center of Newport with its social, theatrical, and athletic activities and helped usher in a new era of social life. As the Gay Nineties unfolded, formality and lavish entertainment came into vogue, and balls and banquets replaced the intimate dinners and high teas of an earlier time.

Kingscote (c. 1850) is on the right side of the avenue just past the Bellevue Shopping Center. William King purchased Kingscote in 1863, after making his fortune in shipbuilding, real estate and the China trade. However, shortly after buying the house, King went insane and spent his remaining years in a mental hospital. Control of the house passed to family members who named it "Kingscote" (King's cottage) and added an additional wing in 1882.

In 1895, the British ambassador to the United States rented Kingscote and used it as his summer residence. During this time, "summer embassies" were common in Newport. Cossack guards stood in front of Stone Villa, the Russian "summer embassy", just north of Kingscote.

Richard Upjohn, the founder of the American Institute of Architects, designed the original Kingscote, and McKim, Mead and White designed the 1882 addition. Upjohn is well known for his Gothic revival style and was responsible for several churches including Trinity in New York and Saint Mary's in Portsmouth, Rhode Island.

Gothic Revival Kingscote, with its asymmetrical and irregular exterior lines, trimmed gables and dormers, and frieze-bordered roof edges, presents a charming and romantic image. The Gothic windows, variety of external forms and rich detail contribute to this picture. The best view of the house is from the weeping willow tree at the edge of the circular drive.

The interior contains many of the same Gothic Revival features found on the outside: arches, columns, intricate woodwork and variety in the size and shape of the rooms. The most ornate and unusual room is the McKim, Mead and White dining room with mahogany paneling, cherrywood floor, Tiffany glass-tiled walls and cork ceiling. In 1972, The Preservation Society of Newport County inherited Kingscote and opened it to the public.

Berkeley Villa is diagonally across the avenue, at the corner with Bowery Street. This Colonial Revival mansion (also known as Bellevue House) was built in 1910 for heiress Martha Codman. She later married singer and famous art collector Maxim Karolik, who was thirty years her junior. Karolik grew up in Russia and claimed to have heard of only three American cities: Washington, New York and Newport. He described his boyhood image: "I didn't know much about Washington, and I thought there were Indians in New York, but I did know one thing-- that American millionaires spent their summers in castles in Newport." The couple spent twenty happy years in this house. Note the Corinthian columns supporting the portico.

Continue down the avenue and look for **Elmcourt** (built in 1853) on the right side, opposite Berkeley Avenue. This brick Tuscan Revival villa, with its extensive landscaping, was one of the first on the Avenue. The Duchess de Dino once lived here in the 1800s, but for much of the Gilded Age it was owned by Wall Street tycoon, Frank Work.

Berkeley House (1884-85), on the corner with Berkeley Avenue, is a brick Queen Anne style cottage designed by Stanford White for Leroy King. Architectural features such as the mosaic-like imbedded stones above the door and on one of the dormers; the combination of stone, brick and wood; and the variety of window shapes are similar to the Samuel Tilton House (see Victorian tour), another Stanford White design.

Berkeley House

46

Edna Villa (1882-83) is on the right, next to Elm Court. Designed by McKim, Mead and White, this cottage with its sweeping porches and diverse shingle patterns is a fine example of shingle-style architecture. James Gordon Bennett built Edna Villa for his sister, Mrs. Isaac Bell, Jr.

Back on the left, look for the **Baldwin House** (1877-78), a huge Queen Anne Revival combining brick, clapboard and shingles into a Tudor style, with timbered gables, a penetrating chimney and extending piazzas. The spacious interior hall is richly paneled and vaulted.

On the right side of Bellevue Avenue, just before Dixon Street, is a massive stone mansion called **The Elms**. In 1901, Philadelphia architect Horace Trumbauer designed The Elms for coal baron Julius Berwind. Trumbauer modeled The Elms after the Chateau d'Argenson, an 18th century classic French chateau. The lavish interior decoration is the work of the renowned House of Alavoine of Paris. Nouveau riche Berwind, the son of poor German immigrants, made his fortune through his own efforts. In 1874, Berwind with his three brothers established a coal mining company which later became the dominant supplier to the United States Merchant Marine and Navy. Coal fueled the Industrial Revolution, and at one point the Berwinds owned 260,000 acres of coal land.

The Elms

Although Berwind lived and worked in New York, he became a weekend commuter during the summer season, sailing on the Fall River steamer to Newport on Fridays and returning to New York on Sunday evenings. A servant staff of twelve to sixteen cared for the Berwinds in their summer "cottage." Usually the Berwinds entertained on a comparatively small scale, but the ball to inaugurate the opening of The Elms was a lavish affair. It was probably the most spectacular party of the 1901 season, with extensive floral decorations, three orchestras, 125 couples and pet monkeys running over the lawn.

Following the French classical style, symmetry, balance and clarity are integral characteristics of The Elms. The interior is exquisitely adorned with elegant objects of art, lavish ornamentation on the walls and ceilings, authentic Louis XIV and XV furniture and splendid paintings loaned by the Metropolitan Museum of Art.

The ornate ballroom with curved corners presents a pleasing, flowing image to the eye. The opposing mirrors are interesting with their endless mutual reflections. The fabulous grand staircase is made of white marble and limestone. The bedrooms are small in comparison to their European counterparts--reflective of their use only during a short summer season. The terrace, lawn and sunken garden exhibit horticultural excellence in the variety of plantings and meticulous design. The servants were quartered in a hidden sixteen-room third story. Note the statuary placed along the roof line.

Berwind's sister Julia last occupied the house until she died in 1961. Then the Preservation Society of Newport County purchased The Elms and opened it as a museum, preserved for public viewing.

De la Salle (1882-84), the William Weld mansion, is directly across the avenue from The Elms. Architect Dudley Newton designed this granite Gothic-style castle, which was a long-time Catholic boys school and is now condominiums. Continue along Bellevue Avenue, and on the left just past Parker Avenue, you'll find **Wayside**, a brick Colonial Revival mansion and former residence of Gilded Age raconteur, Elisha Dyer.

White Lodge, the home of Lispenard Stewart, is next in line. This elegant villa had a Nile-green ballroom and a beautifully paneled dining room ornamented with delicate Gothic scrolls. New York lawyer Lispenard Stewart was the most sought after bachelor in Newport. Trim, courtly and conceited, Stewart was the epitome of Gilded Age gallantry. However, Stewart met his match in the rich (sugar fortune) and beautiful Mrs. Henry O. Havemeyer, Jr. She created a tense scene at one of Alva Belmont's Marble House balls when, although escorted by Stewart, she spent the entire evening gossiping with friends. Stewart maintained his cool but vowed never to talk to her again.

After White Lodge on the same side of the avenue, you'll encounter the **C.C. Baldwin House**, inexplicably named Chateau Nooga (1880-81). Windows and timbers abound in this ornate structure, which was also known as the "Chatter Box." A huge gable and a smaller partner dominate the front.

Cross Narragansett Avenue, and you'll find the **William Osgood House** (1887) on the left corner. This rough-cut granite house was once owned by Herbert Pell, the father of Senator Claiborne Pell. The building formerly housed Saint Catherine's, a girls high school, and it's now owned by the Preservation Society of Newport County. **Rockry Hall** is on the opposite corner. This stone and shingle Gothic villa was built in 1848 for Albert Sumner. Note the triple-flued chimney in the front.

Continue south to the corner with Webster Street, and look for **Swanhurst**, set back on the right side. Scottish stonemason, Alexander McGregor built this fascinating fortress. The fine masonry walls in this Tuscan Revival villa are entirely obscured by a layer of stucco. McGregor, who also designed Fort Adams, the Perry Mill and the Newport Artillery building, built Swanhurst in 1851 for Judge Swan. Swan's descendent Sallie Whiting gave the house to the Newport Art Museum, and for many years it was and important cultural center.

Go down Bellevue Avenue to Hazard Avenue. The two estates on each side of Hazard Avenue once belonged to the renowned Brown family, the benefactors of Brown University. The **Harold Brown House** on the north side, is a Gothic villa designed in 1894 by Dudley Newton. The English-style landscaping is the work on the famed Olmsted firm, the designers of New York's Central Park. The entrance gate is just before Hazard Avenue, but you have to go down Hazard Avenue to get a good view of this house. The vast lawn has several great big trees. The south-side mansion is a wooden Victorian once owned by **John Carter Brown**. The rounded portico matches a similar roof line topped by a romantic cupola.

Chateau-sur-Mer sits on the opposite side of Bellevue Avenue, set way back. This formidable but picturesque granite castle was built in the Victorian style and sharply contrasts (and pre-dates) the more ornate Gilded Age palaces found in this area. Chateau-sur-Mer was the most substantial and impressive Newport "cottage" when it was built in 1852 (and enlarged in 1872). At one time the property line extended to the ocean, hence the name Chateau-sur-Mer which means "castle by the sea."

The ballroom was the first of significance in Newport. In 1857, the *fete champetre*, given by owner William Wetmore, attracted an estimated 2,500 guests. This event, which presaged the gala turn-of-century balls, was the entertainment "benchmark" for Newport after the Civil War.

For generations, the Wetmore family was a prominent part of Newport. William Wetmore got rich in the China trade, and his son, George Peabody Wetmore was a powerful Rhode Island politician (governor and United States Senator). The daughters of George Wetmore, Edith and Maude, were leading Newport socialites and philanthropists. Edith Wetmore along with Mrs. John Jacob Astor pioneered the game of women's tennis at the Newport Casino when they daringly wore white tennis shoes, black stockings, white silk blouses and pleated skirts with bloomers. The outfits were topped with sailor hats, over double veils to protect delicate faces from the summer sun.

The atrium-like central hall is Chateau-sur-Mer's most striking feature, rising forty-five feet to a glass ceiling and skylight and surrounded by balconies on each floor. The Italian decorator, Frulini, designed much of the interior, such as the walnut library, finely carved in Renaissance style. The carvings in the Frulini dining room extol the sensual pleasures of eating and drinking in Bacchic (god of wine) tradition. Underneath the stairs, the painted Tree of Life rises three stories to a ceiling decorated with birds and a blue sky.

Outside, the irregular Victorian lines, high mansard roof and rough granite walls present a harsh, sharp appearance. The huge weeping beech across from the entrance, with branches touching the ground, gives an explorer the feeling of walking through a forest.

Continue across Shepard Avenue and look for **Vernon Court** on the left side. Mrs. Richard Gambrill, an influential widowed socialite, reigned from this majestic French Provincial chateau, designed for lavish entertainment by architect Thomas Hastings (New York Public

Chateau-sur-Mer

Vernon Court

Fairlawn

Library) in 1901. White stuccoed walls, heavily ornamented in terra cotta, and an enormous multi-chimneyed roof are prominent features of this sophisticated structure. The grand formal grounds include a copy of Henry VIII's garden for Anne Boleyn. You can get an excellent view of the estate from Victoria Avenue, look through the large iron gate in the back.

Continue on the left sidewalk to Ruggles Avenue, and you'll come to **Fairlawn** (c.1852). In 1883, the estate was owned by Levi Morton, who was Vice President of the United States in the Benjamin Harrison administration and Governor of New York. At the turn of the century, Scottish multi-millionaire I. Townsend Burden owned this Elizabethan brick and brownstone estate. Mrs. Burden was the socialite responsible for inviting fellow Baltimorean Harry Lehr to Newport, thus launching his bizarre and warped social career. **Belmead**, a three-story brick mansion, is across the avenue.

Continue on the left side, walk past Marine Avenue (dirt road), and look for **Rosecliff** on the edge of the sea. This exquisite mansion was the summer residence of Mr. and Mrs. Hermann Oelrichs. The firm of McKim, Mead and White designed Rosecliff after the Grand Trianon Palace built by Louis XIV in Versailles.

From 1851 to 1891, George Bancroft—noted diplomat, historian, horseman and horticulturist— owned the land now occupied by Rosecliff. Bancroft was the founder of the U.S. Naval Academy and Ambassador to England and Prussia. He is credited with establishing the extensive rose beds for which the property is named.

In 1891, Theresa and Virginia Fair purchased the Rosecliff property for $140,000. Theresa and Virginia (affectionately known as Tessie and Birdie) were the daughters of James Fair, an Irish immigrant who made a fortune by striking the largest vein in the Comstock Lode (one of the largest gold and silver deposits ever discovered). However, immense power and wealth unleashed the dark side of James Fair, and he became an accomplished practitioner of avarice, corruption and blatant debauchery. He cheated in business, ran a successful but corrupt campaign for U.S. Senator from Nevada, and was an extensive womanizer. Fair gave Tessie a million dollars when she married Hermann Oelrichs, a wealthy New York businessman. After his eventual divorce and death, Fair's enormous wealth passed to his two daughters. Tessie built the existing Rosecliff mansion in 1900 and became one of the outstanding hostesses of Newport society.

Rosecliff is H-shaped with two partially enclosed terraces. The garden terrace, an 18th century French Court of Love, was patterned after one built for Marie Antoinette. The first floor, used for entertaining, is about twenty feet high, while the second floor (bedrooms) is only ten feet. The concealed third floor was used for servants' quarters. The exterior is covered with white terra cotta, a fired clay that looks like stone.

The intention was entertainment on a grand scale, as seen in the spacious first floor design. Rooms and doors are arranged to permit the smooth movement of many people. The most striking feature of the interior is the spectacular curving marble staircase, which gracefully flows in a heart-shaped pattern. Other notable features are the massive archway leading into the stair hall, and the walls and ceilings (particularly in the ballroom), which are extravagantly adorned with carved and molded plaster fashioned into rococo designs.

The south rose garden, restored in 1976, has paths paved with marble chips and contains 180 plants. In 1973, scenes for the movie The Great Gatsby were filmed at Rosecliff. The Preservation Society of Newport County operates Rosecliff and provides guided tours.

The **Sherwood** mansion (1904), the former home of Mr. and Mrs. Pembroke Jones, is across the avenue from Rosecliff. In the rarefied air of the strictly closed Newport society, the Joneses were successful social climbers from North Carolina. Mr. Jones was a rice baron who rapidly penetrated High Society after relocating to New York. In Newport, the social gatecrashers set up housekeeping in this magnificent mansion.

The Joneses overcame objections from Newport's Old Guard by throwing lavish Southern dinners and entertaining in grand style. Mrs. Jones regularly earmarked $300,000 for entertainment at the beginning of each Newport season. For one party, they thought nothing of building an eighty-five by forty foot, completely enclosed outdoor ballroom and theater, decorated with floor-to-ceiling plate glass mirrors and 10,000 water lilies. Contrary to Newport's social norms, Pembroke Jones was always ready with a hearty laugh, a ribald joke or a pre-lunch mint julep.

According to legend, the fabulously wealthy Palm Beach real estate baron and Standard Oil founder, Henry Flagler, met the love of his life, Mary Lily Kenan, while visiting Sherwood. In Cinderella tradition, Mary Lily was a poor relative of the Joneses and a shy recluse who spent her days upstairs sewing, until discovered by Flagler. As Flagler's young wife, she would later inherit an enormous sum and go on to become a most powerful and influential woman.

Sherwood is an expansive Georgian mansion, with a huge columned portico and several similarities to the "White House."

Beechwood is on the left side, a little farther down Bellevue Avenue, past Bancroft Avenue. During the Gay Nineties, Caroline Astor, the queen of American society, held summer court from the lovely Beechwood mansion. Mrs. Astor originated the exalted "List of 400" (the social elite who dominated Newport society) and later went on to become a near cult figure ruling over social climbers with an iron hand.

This charming stuccoed brick mansion is bordered on three sides by a spacious piazza. The elegant and tasteful Beechwood, built in 1852, sharply contrasts with the overpowering marble palaces that dominate Bellevue Avenue. You can tour Beechwood and be treated to a lively theatrical performance that will sweep you back to the turn of the century. As Mrs. Astor's invited guest, you'll be guided by a colorful entourage and gaze into the fascinating Gilded Age of Newport. The description of the mansion and Newport society is humorous and enlightening.

Rosecliff

Beechwood

Marble House

Marble House, the magnificent William K. Vanderbilt mansion, is next to Beechwood. Marble House is most famous for its former mistress, the indomitable Alva Vanderbilt Belmont, a leader of Newport society and one of the most powerful American women of her time. Alva teamed up with Tessie Oelrichs (Rosecliff) and Mamie Fish (Crossways) to form "The Great Triumvirate", a formidable troika that set social standards for Newport society. In 1895, Alva stunned High Society when she divorced William K. Vanderbilt and married his good friend Perry Belmont (Belcourt Castle). She later became a leader of the women's suffrage movement, casting her enormous influence and wealth into the effort.

Marble House opened in 1892 and secured for Newport the leadership of the American Renaissance in classical architecture. Richard Morris Hunt designed Marble House and supervised construction over a four-year period. Patterned after the Trianon at Versailles, this most sumptuous residence has an imposing two-story entrance portico supported by gigantic fluted Corinthian columns. Ornamental columns surround the house, which is bordered by a roof-top balustrade. The ornate entrance grille weighs over ten tons. Its doors are set on pivots (instead of hinges) and close to a perfect fit. The entrance hall rises over twenty feet and is lined with yellow Italian marble. The bronze fountain and lamp standards (monogrammed "W.V.," for William Vanderbilt) were made by the French interior decorating firm of J. Allard, whose work can be seen throughout Marble House. The bronze Allard chairs and stools in the dining room are believed to be the only examples of bronze furniture in the world.

Throughout the house, the ornamentation is abundant with scenes and figures from Greek and Roman mythology. The rooms exhibit a variety of styles. The elegant dining room is faced with dark pink Numidian marble from Africa, while the Gothic Room and the rococo-style library contrast sharply with the Gold Room, which is a stunning display of gilt.

After her divorce, Alva closed Marble House and moved down the avenue to govern Belcourt Castle. She reopened Marble House in 1913 and hosted a large garden party and suffrage rally. The Preservation Society of Newport County now owns the mansion and gives guided tours.

Across the avenue, **Champ Soleil** hides amidst the trees in apparent contradiction to its sunny name. Mrs. Drexel Dahlgren, of the Main Line Philadelphia Drexels, built this profusely landscaped French Provincial estate in 1929. Look through iron gate (note the Sun King emblem) to this elegant mansion with its steeply pitched roof and smart symmetrical lines.

Back on the left side, walk past **Felicity** to **Beaulieu**, a sturdy mansion bordering Cliff Walk and overlooking the sea. Beaulieu, built in 1859 for the Peruvian ambassador to the United States, has seen more than its share of Gilded Age barons. James Gordon Bennett, William Waldorf Astor, Cornelius Vanderbilt III and legendary hostess Grace Wilson Vanderbilt made Beaulieu their summer residence. The mansion has a charming French concave (mansard style) roof, densely bricked walls and a deep seaside verandah.

Keeping walking southward, and you'll soon see **Clarendon Court**. Horace Trumbauer (The Elms) designed this 18th century English mansion in 1904. Edward Knight, a Pennsylvania Railroad executive, was the original owner, but Clarendon Court has seen several other prominent residents, including Maysie Rovensky, whose son Philip Plant is remembered as the husband of actress Constance Bennett. Allegedly, Plant's rakish lifestyle was responsible for the coining of the word "playboy." The Rovenskys bequeathed Rovensky Park, across the avenue from the mansion.

However, the most well known owners of Clarendon Court were surely Claus and Martha "Sunny" von Bulow. Claus was twice tried for the attempted murder of his heiress wife, after she lapsed into an irreversible coma resulting from insulin injections. He was convicted but then acquitted on appeal. Following a lawsuit by Sunny's children, Claus agreed to give up his rights to Clarendon Court and his wife's inheritance. Clarendon Court is another study in symmetry and manicured landscaping.

Take a moment here to relax on one of the benches in **Rovensky Park**. You'll enjoy viewing the grounds, and if you're feet are up to it, stroll the winding paths.

Back on the left side again, walk past Clarendon Court to adjoining **Miramar**, another Horace Trumbauer work. Mrs. George Widener of Philadelphia built Miramar in 1914. The mansion is set in extensive formal gardens and is a model of classical architecture and rigidity. In 1912, the year construction began on Miramar, Mr. Widener and his son perished on the Titanic. Mrs. Widener later married noted explorer Dr. Alexander Hamilton Rice. Balls at Miramar were legendary, particularly during Tennis Week. In the Newport tradition, they lasted all night, but Mrs. Rice would nap shortly after midnight and return refreshed just before breakfast to greet the revelers. Mrs. Widener established the Widener Library at Harvard University.

Walk across the avenue and continue past Lakeview Avenue. Look on the right for the iron gate of **Belcourt Castle**, the former home of Oliver Hazard Perry ("Perry") Belmont and his wife, Alva Vanderbilt Belmont. Belmont built this castle (for about $3 million) in 1894, two years before he married the former Mrs. William K. Vanderbilt, the ex-mistress of Marble House. The new Mrs. Belmont was one of Newport's great hostesses, and Belcourt became the scene of many fabulous balls.

Oliver's father, August Belmont, established the family fortune in banking and later married the daughter of Commodore Matthew Perry, thus linking the Belmont fortune with the prestigious Newport naval family, the Perrys. August built one of the early Bellevue Avenue mansions, the now-demolished "By-the-Sea" located near Marine Avenue, next to Rosecliff.

The Belmonts entertained extensively. Belcourt guests included the Duke of Windsor and Kaiser Wilhelm. Even lunch could be lavish, and Mrs. Belmont was known to invite friends from nearby Bailey's Beach back to the castle for a midday buffet of lobster, ham and turkey. The Belmont family loved horses. Perry Belmont couldn't bear to be too far from them, so his were lodged on the first floor of

Champ Soleil

Clarendon Court

Belcourt Castle

Belcourt. The Belmonts helped build Belmont Park horse track in New York.

Prolific mansion architect, Richard Morris Hunt designed Belcourt and supervised construction over a three-year period. This sixty-room castle, patterned after a Louis XIII hunting lodge at Versailles, contains the largest collection of 13th-century stained glass in America. Antiques and art treasures abound in this eclectic museum. Oriental rugs (over 100), exquisite Renaissance furniture and paintings, and all sorts of armor and urns adorn the castle. The interior design of the castle reflects French influence, particularly from the 16th century.

The Grand Hall, guarded by two imposing Italian marble columns, contains innumerable Chinese art work and an 18th-century bronze statue of Apollo. Apollo appears again in the dining room driving his sun chariot along the ceiling. There's also indirect lighting designed by Belmont's friend, Thomas Edison. The archetypical Gothic ballroom is an amalgamation of vaulting stained-glass windows and columns. The room contains an extensive armor collection, 15th-century German throne chairs, and a great fireplace that looks like a castle. Belcourt was built for endurance; the brick and granite exterior walls are forty-two inches thick, and the castle sits on a four-foot thick concrete block.

The Tinney family now owns Belcourt Castle, and they have opened this spectacular museum for public touring.

Across the avenue, you'll see **Ocean View**, a distinguished mansard-roofed wooden house built in 1856. Mr. and Mrs. Ogden Mills lived here during the Gilded Age. The Mills were old line aristocrats who entertained in a formal, stately fashion. Mrs. Mills claimed she could give a party for a hundred without calling in extra help. But she was much too self-important and strait-laced to gain popularity among the more hedonistic Gilded Agers. Ogden Mills was secretary of the Treasury during the Hoover administration.

Just past Ocean View, Bellevue Avenue turns ninety degrees to the right. **Rough Point**, the Doris Duke mansion, is at the point of this elbow. The stone and barbed-wire wall, imposing metal gate and ominous sound of guard dogs are apt barriers protecting the recluse residing in this Gothic mansion. You'll find a more detailed description of Rough Point in the Cliff Walk tour.

Roselawn is on the inside of the elbow opposite Rough Point. Mrs. J.F. Pierson lived in this "carpenter Gothic" villa, with its multi-gabled roof and spacious porches. Continue along the right side of Bellevue Avenue, and opposite Ledge Road you'll find **Inchquin**, a rough-cut granite French Renaissance villa. **Beachmound** is the next and last house on Bellevue Avenue. Built in 1897 for Pittsburg's Benjamin Thaw, this Colonial Revival mansion has a huge pillared portico and a great view of Bailey's Beach.

This concludes the Bellevue Avenue tour, but if you're driving or riding a bicycle, you can pick up the Ocean Drive tour at this point.

Ochre Point

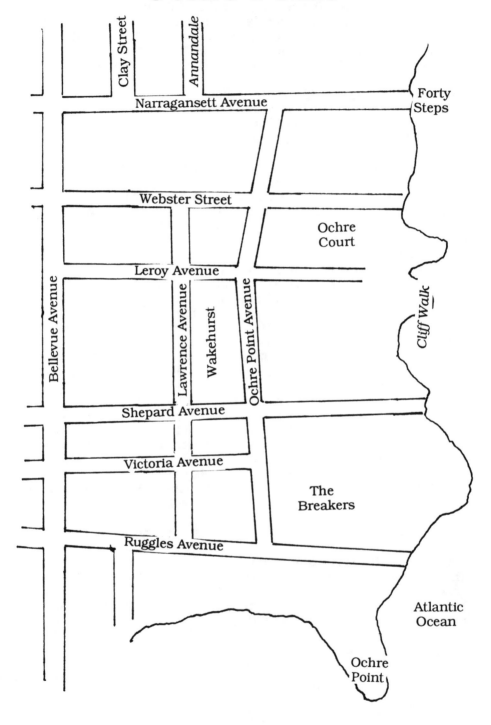

GILDED NEWPORT
Ochre Point

HIGHLIGHTS - On this tour, you can explore the grounds and the interiors of several important and interesting Gilded Age mansions. The Preservation Society of Newport County owns The Breakers mansion and offers an extensive tour for a reasonable charge. Salve Regina University owns several historic mansions and permits visitors to the first floor of Ochre Court and Wakehurst at no charge.

The Ochre Point section consists roughly of the area between Bellevue Avenue and Cliff Walk, bounded by Narragansett Avenue on the north and Ruggles Avenue on the south. Ochre Point was named for the reddish brown tint of the clay found along the cliffs on the edge of the Atlantic Ocean.

The Ochre Point tour begins at the corner of Narragansett Avenue and Bellevue Avenue and ends where Ruggles Avenue joins Bellevue Avenue about a half-mile to the south.

Go east on Narragansett Avenue, toward the ocean. This broad street is lined with several grand Gilded Age "cottages". On the left just before Clay Street, you'll find **Gravel Court**, a Gothic cottage with a slight French accent built in the 1870s. The twin gables on either side of center contrast with a central gable on the other side (which is actually the front).

Look for **Bois Dore** (c. 1927) on the right side of the street, behind the pink stucco wall. This elegant limestone French chateau with its vast grounds was originally the home of Pennsylvania's William Fahnestock, who was known to hang 14-carat gold fruit from the trees of the estate. Bois Dore is now the home of oil heiress Caroline Skelly. Through the years the mansion has seen some notable jewel thefts. Twin guardhouses stand at the entrance to a driveway lined with meticulously pruned trees. Note the exquisite elliptical window above the portico and the twin chimneys of this symmetrical mansion.

Back on the other side of the Avenue, just after Clay Street, you'll find **Chepstow**, a late 19th century cottage with a flared mansard roof, white brick walls and broad sweeping grounds decorated with superb trees.

Continue along the left side, past **Starboard House**, **Narragansett House** and the **Pinard Cottages**. **Bienvenue** is on the right side, opposite the Pinard Cottages. Built in the style of an Italian villa, this three-story cottage (c.1854) was the summer home of Joseph Hart, a Troy, New York industrialist. The belvedere entrance tower dominates a facade of flush-lapped clapboards which look like stone. The main house and the adjoining carriage house have now been converted to condominiums.

Walk along Narragansett Avenue, across Annandale Road toward Cliff Walk. **The Orchard** is set back behind the iron gate on the left, just a block from the sea. This mansion was built in 1871 and is an exact copy, formal grounds and all, of an 18th century French country house. During the Gilded Age, the house was owned by Colonel George Fearing.

Turn right and go down Ochre Point Avenue. **Southside**, an 1882 Queen Anne cottage, is at the corner of Narragansett Avenue and Ochre Point Avenue. This mansion is mostly hidden on this side by huge rhododendron bushes and is best viewed from Cliff Walk (it's described in more detail on that tour). Continue south on Ochre Point Avenue across Webster Street, and the next summer cottage you'll see is the ornate **Ochre Court**, the former home of Mr. and Mrs. Ogden Goelet. Ochre Court is a fifty-room French chateau built in 1888 for Ogden Goelet, a wealthy New York real estate developer. Author Blanche Oelrichs describes Goelet as a man who worked himself to death. She recalls seeing Goelet shuffling around the grounds of Ochre Court on the arm of his nurse. She was told Goelet could digest practically nothing but grapes. Mrs. Goelet, on the other hand, became a most pursued widow. Enormously rich, arrogant and calculating, she entertained lavishly and lived in gilded splendor behind the gates.

Architect Richard Morris Hunt modeled Ochre Court after Edward VII's castle in Paris. The design exhibits rounded arches, balconies, high roofs, turrets and tall chimneys. Other exterior features include sandstone carvings of gargoyles, griffins and relaxing workmen. The south wall even has a sundial. On the grounds, you'll find a colorful oriental Dogwood and a Copper Beech tree.

The Great Hall in Ochre Court rises three stories and is surrounded by an ornate balconied gallery. The ceiling features a banquet out of Roman mythology, and the Caen stone walls exhibit a myriad of symbolic carvings including dolphins, salamanders and cherubs. The medieval stained glass window on the street side beside the grand staircase shows God the Father, the Devil and other religious symbolism.

In 1947, Goelet's son Robert donated the mansion to the Catholic Diocese of Providence, and it is now the administrative center for Salve Regina University.

Most of this area is the Salve Regina campus. Across from Ochre Court, you'll see two shingle style cottages joined by a large wooden central archway. Formerly the carriage house for **Whiteholme**, the Henry Barton Jacobs mansion, this turn-of-century building is all that remains of the magnificent estate, which was located at the corner of Narragansett Avenue and Ochre Point Avenue.

Keeping walking along Ochre Point Avenue, across Leroy Avenue. **Vinland**, the former Twombly estate, is essentially the block to the left of Ochre Point Avenue between Leroy Avenue and Shepard Avenue. The main house on the grounds is a brownstone Queen Anne villa built in 1883. Vinland is the former summer home of Mrs. Hamilton McKown Twombly, the last of the great Newport *grande dames*. Mrs. Twombly, the last grandchild of Commodore Cornelius Vanderbilt, presided over Vinland for more than fifty years, before she died in 1952 at the age of ninety-eight. Mrs. Twombly's sumptuous dinners included the finest French cuisine, and her French chef

Ochre Court

Wakehurst

Seaview

became wealthy enough to retire in his own Newport cottage. When she rode cross-country in her Rolls Royce to attend her grandson's wedding, the careful Mrs. Twombly dressed as a maid and sat in front with the chauffeur, while the maid rode in the back disguised as the Madame.

Explore the meticulously landscaped grounds of this Romanesque style estate. Notice the heavy rusticated stone and the floral motif around the windows of the fifty-room main house. There's a huge Roman pot near the entrance. It was given to the original owners in 1884 and is believed to date from 200 AD. You can relax in the rose garden and enjoy a great view of the ocean. Check out the enormous Fernleaf Beech in front of the mansion. In the late 1800s, this tree was shipped from Yonkers New York to Newport harbor and pulled by oxen to the estate.

Other notable buildings on the estate are the **carriage house** (once attached to the main house and later moved in a laudable engineering feat), the **caretaker's cottage** (a 1907 Colonial Revival) and the mini-turreted **gatehouse** where the gardener lived (notice the elaborate wrought-iron lantern).

At one point, the estate had more than fifteen automobiles, all painted in Vanderbilt maroon. The Boston architectural firm of Peabody and Stearns designed the mansion and attendant buildings. Salve Regina University now owns the estate and has renamed the main house McAuley Hall in honor of the first Sister of Mercy, Catherine McAuley.

From the gatehouse, walk across Ochre Point Avenue to another block-sized estate, **Wakehurst**. You can enter the estate by the path in the middle of the block. The main house is to the right near the back and the carriage house is on the left bordering Shepard Avenue. The other building in between is the new Salve Regina library. Notice the beautiful trees on this estate, particularly the huge Weeping Beech on the southwest lawn and the broad London Plane Tree on the southeast lawn.

The Wakehurst mansion is a fascinating copy of an English country manor house. At first glance, it seems almost a mini Elizabethan castle, lording over an English estate, but it's really a charming stone Tudor mansion. English architect Charles Kempe designed Wakehurst, patterning it after Wakehurst Place in England, and renowned American architect Dudley Newton supervised the building process. The rooms were imported from England and reassembled in the mansion. The exterior is striking with its multiple gables, ball-topped pinnacles, diamond-paned window bands and stone sculpturing.

Wakehurst is the former home of James Van Alen, a railroad heir who married Mrs. Caroline Astor's daughter, Emily. After his wife died, Van Alen became one of Newport's most eligible bachelors. Van Alen was a consummate Anglophile, adorning the mansion with English tapestries, high-backed oak benches, dower chests, grandfather clocks and pewter tankards. Eccentrically, Van Alen even flavored his vocabulary with such Tudor period expressions as "egad", "zounds", "varlet" and "wench." Van Alen was firmly established at the upper crust of Newport society. He was a connoisseur of food and wine, and his musicales and parties were the height of fashion. The mansion is now the Salve Regina campus center.

Walk behind the Wakehurst mansion and go through the back entrance to Lawrence Avenue. Salve Regina's **Mercy Hall** (c. 1886) is across the street. This charming Queen Anne style carriage house originally housed the stables for Ochre Court. The multi-gabled red brick exterior is neatly trimmed in white and topped by a classic stable tower. Mercy Hall is the campus arts center and contains the cozy Megley Theatre and the McKillop Gallery.

Wetmore Stables (c. 1852) is next to Mercy Hall. It's the former carriage house for Chateau-sur-Mer and was design by Newport renaissance man George Champlin Mason.

Walk southward on Lawrence Avenue and turn right on Shepard Avenue. You'll soon come to the imposing **William Watts Sherman House** on the left side. This classic Queen Anne style Tudor manor house was built in 1874 for New York banker William Watts Sherman. The Watts Sherman House, designed by H. H. Richardson (Boston's Trinity Church), was the premier American model and trendsetter for shingle style architecture. The exterior, dominated by two enormous gables set at right angles, builds from a stone base into a rich texture of shingles arrayed in intricate patterns, small-paned bay windows and half-timbering set in terra-cotta stucco. The interior has a spacious central hall with a great free-standing fireplace, exquisite paneling, ornate wood carvings, beamed ceilings and La Farge stained glass. In total, three renowned American architects had a hand in Watts Sherman, as a later addition was designed by Dudley Newton, and Stanford White redecorated several rooms. The Watts Sherman House is now a Salve Regina residence hall.

Turn around and walk back along Shepard Avenue, past Lawrence Avenue to Ochre Point Avenue, turn right and go along the gravel sidewalk. **The Breakers** estate is on the left side, behind a formidable iron wall with large stone pillars.

The Breakers is the most fabulous and massive of all Newport mansions. In 1892, Cornelius Vanderbilt II commissioned Richard Morris Hunt to design this spectacular and imposing mansion. Cornelius II was the oldest son of William Henry Vanderbilt and grandson of family founder Commodore Cornelius Vanderbilt. Along with his brother, William K. Vanderbilt (see Marble House), Cornelius inherited the bulk of the family fortune. He took over leadership of the New York Central and Michigan Central railroads. Cornelius was a diligent workaholic and a stern, solemn, seemingly ascetic man (didn't smoke or drink). He had a penchant for charitable and religious activities and donated much of his income and time to this effort. Cornelius wasn't given to frivolity, and he shunned society in favor of teaching Sunday school and working as a church vestryman. Cornelius was heavily involved in Newport life, principally as a pillar of the community. Yet ironically he is best known for creating The Breakers, a mansion that clashed so much with his phlegmatic personality. For Cornelius, The Breakers was the ultimate paradox. It was by far the most lavish and ostentatious private residence in Newport, if not the world. The only reasonable explanation for this incongruity lies with Alice Claypoole Gwynne, Cornelius' wife.

By the late 1880s, Alice Vanderbilt entered into a bitter rivalry with Alva Vanderbilt (William K.'s wife) for social leadership of the Vanderbilt family. The indomitable Alva had Alice outgunned when it came to manipulation and maneuvering, but as the wife of the head of the Vanderbilt family, Alice was not about to capitulate. And her ace in the hole was The Breakers.

Certainly architect Hunt must have consulted extensively with Alice, since The Breakers with it's breathtaking opulence was so out of character for Cornelius. Hunt chose the European Renaissance style, modeling the mansion after a Northern Italian villa and amazingly took only two years to build it. The project was a tremendous undertaking and included a workforce of hundreds of laborers and craftsmen, many imported from Europe.

In France, craftsmen assembled (down to the last detail) the Grand Salon, which was then disassembled, crated and shipped to Newport. Then to ensure perfection, the same French craftsmen traveled to Newport and reassembled the room in The Breakers. Fearing fire, Hunt used no wood in construction, only steel beams, stone, brick and tile. For the interior he imported marble, alabaster and stone from Europe and Africa.

The Breakers

The entrance is guarded by enormous, but perfectly balanced oak doors. Weighing many tons, they still move at the slight push of a finger. Behind the oak doors, between the vestibule and the entrance hall, are a pair of huge hand-wrought, iron-grilled doors paneled with plate glass and weighing over seventy tons.

The Great Hall in the center of the mansion is awesome. It rises forty-five feet through two full floors to a ceiling painted to look like a blue cloud-dotted sky. Carvings and marble plaques adorn walls faced with French Caen stone, and huge fluted pilasters decorate the perimeter, with carved acorns and oak leaves (the Vanderbilt symbol) abounding. The rooms on the second floor open onto balconies overlooking the Great Hall. A grand circular staircase, with fountain beneath, divides at a landing and rises gracefully to a balcony. A huge (twenty-four by eighteen feet) Flemish tapestry overlooks the landing.

The billiard room, made of pale-green Cippolino marble from floor-to-ceiling, is trimmed in mahogany and contains an English weighing chair that gives the weight of the sitter in stones.

The most lavish and ornate room is probably the dining room. A ceiling painting of Aurora at Dawn overlooks this spacious two-story room, which is surrounded by twelve massive red Numidian marble columns. Two enormous chandeliers hang from a ceiling containing life-size figures set into arches.

The exterior of this stone palace, sitting high above the ocean, exhibits double loggias (open galleries) with different-size arches, ornamental marble columns, and a variety of towers and terraces. The renowned Olmsted firm of landscape architects designed the grounds. The house has seventy rooms, with thirty-three for the servants on a hidden fourth floor.

Cornelius Vanderbilt II died in 1899 at age fifty-six. Many said he worked himself to death with worry over the railroads, numerous charities and family responsibilities. Most people were unaware of the extent of his charitable involvement. Even though he spent and gave away vast amounts of his fortune, Cornelius still managed to increase his initial inheritance. His estate amounted to almost $73 million. His second son Alfred received the bulk of the estate (almost $43 million). His estranged eldest son Neily was virtually cut out. His wife Alice inherited a $7 million trust fund, and of course, she got The Breakers. After her husband's death, Alice settled into the role of family matriarch and had a long reign at The Breakers, becoming an institution in Newport's social scene. She died in 1934 at age eighty-nine.

The Breakers is now owned by the Preservation Society of Newport County and is open for public viewing.

Continue down Ochre Point Avenue, and at the end of the street, across Ruggles Avenue, you'll encounter **Fairholme**, a large Tudor villa with a medieval half-timbered facade. Fairholme (c.1870), designed by architects Furness and Hewitt, was originally the home of Fairman Rogers of Philadelphia. Rogers was the author of the authoritative manual on coaching. The Drexel family later owned Fairholme, but Mr. and Mrs. Robert Young were probably the most famous owners. Railroader Robert Young (of Newport, Palm Beach and White Sulphur Springs) was the tycoon who wrested the reins of the New York Central from the Vanderbilt family. Mrs. Young, the sister of famed artist Georgia O'Keeffe, often entertained the Duke and Duchess of Windsor at Fairholme.

Turn right and walk westward on Ruggles Avenue toward Bellevue Avenue. **Ochre Lodge** (c. 1895) is on the right. This gambrel-roofed cottage, designed by Dudley Newton, combines a stone base with shingled upper floors. On the other side of the street, you'll find **Midcliff** (1886), the former home of Oklahoma oil heiress, Minister to Luxembourg, and hostess *par excellence*, Pearl Mesta. She entertained Dwight Eisenhower and Hoover's vice president, Charles Curtis at Midcliff. Midcliff is followed by **Honeysuckle Lodge** (1886), a rambling Queen Anne cottage and former home of famous golf enthusiast, T. Suffern Tailer. **Nethercliffe**, a three-story stone mansion, is on the other side of the street.

Continue along Ruggles Avenue past Lawrence Avenue, and on the right side you'll come to **Althorpe**, an elegant Colonial Revival cottage built in 1890 and designed by the firm of Peabody and Stearns. Notice the broad verandah, dormer windows and tiny widow's walk on the roof. The house is now called Founders Hall and is part of Salve Regina University. The **Fairholme Carriage House**, next to Althorpe, once belonged to Catherine Pell (U.S. Senator Claiborne Pell's great-grandmother).

Continue toward Bellevue Avenue and just past short Wetmore Avenue on the left side, you'll notice the massive **Seaview Terrace**. Edson Bradley, a Washington, D.C. liquor baron, built Seaview Terrace in the late 1920s. It's patterned after the French Renaissance style of a Norman manor house, with a soft-toned limestone exterior extensively adorned with cornerstones and cornices. This fascinating castle has turreted towers, a myriad of glass-inset windows, gables, gargoyles and all sorts of stone sculpturing. Mr. Bradley filled his house with tapestries, stained glass and an eclectic selection of art treasures. The mansion even had a chapel which seated 150 people. The fifty-four room mansion was one of the last great houses built in Newport. However, it wasn't originally built in Newport, it seems that Bradley had it taken apart in Washington and shipped by railroad to Newport where it was reassembled stone by stone. If you've ever watched the old television series "Dark Shadows", you may recognize the mansion, it was shown in each opening scene. The building is now called Carey mansion and is part of Salve Regina University. Stand on the back terrace overlooking Cliff Walk and enjoy the panoramic sea view.

Continue along Ruggles Avenue to Bellevue Avenue and the end of the tour.

CLIFF WALK

HIGHLIGHTS - The combination of ocean, mansion, wildlife and plant life speaks for itself. Most of the mansions (and their residents) on this tour are described in detail in the Bellevue Avenue or Ochre Point tours.

Winding along the rocky coast of Aquidneck Island, Cliff Walk is a three-mile path yielding spectacular views of the crashing surf on one side and fabulous Gilded Age mansions on the other. Cliff Walk runs from Easton's Beach (northern end) to Bailey's Beach (southern end). The upper path is mostly asphalt and gravel, and much of the way is lined with wild berry bushes. Some parts of the lower (southern) section are quite rocky and the actual path becomes almost invisible at times. But just keep going and the path improves again near the end. While walking Cliff Walk, you must be very careful, particularly where the path skirts the edge of the craggy cliffs, high above the Atlantic Ocean. There have been several injurious falls, some fatal.

You don't have to travel the full length of Cliff Walk. You can leave the path at Narragansett Avenue (at Forty Steps), Webster Street, Shepard Avenue, Ruggles Avenue or Marine Avenue. Any of these streets will take you over to Bellevue Avenue.

Bordering estate owners developed Cliff Walk during the Gilded Age, and it was designated a National Historic Walking Trail in 1976. Look for the plaque at the very beginning of Cliff Walk. It commemorates the walk and lists the names of those who helped improve it, including Claus von Bulow.

The big building at the start of the walk is **Cliff Lawn** (now named Cliff Walk Manor), one of the first great houses built on the cliffs. Cliff Lawn was the home of Winthrop Chanler and was the site of a christening party in 1902 for Chanler's grandson, which was attended by his godfather, President Theodore Roosevelt.

On the left you're overlooking Easton's Beach and Easton's Point, with the Atlantic in the background. Walk along the path to some steps and Cliff Terrace, where you'll see several quaint cottages built around 1870. The **Sea-View Cottages** were part of a large hotel complex, most of which burned down in the 1890s. You'll come to a second set of steps at Seaview Avenue.

Continuing along the path, you'll notice the houses in this area are hard to see due to the heavy vegetation. It's virtually impossible to see them in the summer, unless you have a helicopter. But the winding walk soon comes to **Hopedene**, a brick Colonial Revival "cottage" built in 1902 for Mrs. E. H. G. Slater of Providence. As you come around a corner with Forty Steps on the left, you can glimpse the estate through the pine trees (forget it in the summer). If you want a better view of this house, go over to Easton's Point and look across, it can be clearly seen.

The next virtually obscured house is **Fairlawn**, the Harvey Firestone mansion. This vast Queen Anne cottage (also known as Ocean Lawn)

Cliff Walk

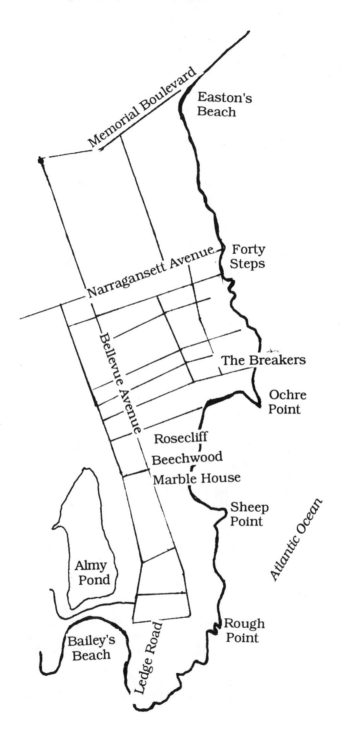

Memorial Boulevard

Easton's
Beach

Narragansett Avenue

Forty
Steps

Bellevue Avenue

The Breakers

Ochre
Point

Rosecliff

Beechwood

Marble House

Sheep
Point

Atlantic Ocean

Almy
Pond

Bailey's
Beach

Ledge Road

Rough
Point

Great Holiday photos of your Best Friends are in the bag!

Bring your Best Friend into
Best Friends Pet Resort & Salon

**Saturday, December 2
& Sunday, December 3
From 3pm to 6pm**

and go home for the holidays with
a great Christmas or Hanukkah
photo of your pet.

**$12 for one full-color 5x7" print.
With all of the proceeds
going to The Cobb County
Humane Society.**

20% OFF
Gifts & Goodies
Retail Sale!

Happy Holidays from your friends at:
Best Friends, Marietta

**1087 Johnson Ferry Rd., N.E.
(678) 560-0880**

Best Friends
PET RESORT & SALON

with ornately carved gothic gables was built for Mrs. William Gammell in 1889. This house is also difficult to see from the walk.

You'll soon come to **Forty Steps** at Narragansett Avenue. The recently restored steps lead down to the rocks and the pounding surf. This is a good place to pause and relax. You can gaze back to Easton's Beach or look toward the great stone mansions of Ochre Court and the Breakers looming ahead. According to tradition, Forty Steps was built in the 1840s by David Priestley Hall to provide easy access to the water. In the late 1800s, native Newporters and mansion domestics gathered here for popular Saturday night dances.

Continue along the rock-lined path through the archway, and you'll come to **Southside**, another Queen Anne cottage, built in 1882. Renowned Gilded Age architects, McKim, Mead and White designed Southside for Robert Goelet of New York. In a storybook romance, Goelet's son Robert married Elsie Whelen, one of the poor but gorgeous Whelen twins. The willowy Elsie became a classic Newport belle--tall and dark with long flowing lines and the picture of grace in a ballroom. Gilded Age author Blanche Oelrichs describes these Newport belles: "How beautifully they stood and moved....with their evening dresses caught up under their breasts, wearing fresh gardenias in their hair, their slim throats encircled by necklaces of emeralds and sapphires." Unfortunately, the couple soon divorced.

This magnificent house is a fine example of shingle-style construction. Intricately arranged shingles, upper-level galleries, a multi-chimneyed roof, and a broad piazza mark the exterior. The interior opens freely around a great hall fireplace. Walk across Webster Street, and continue along the path.

The next summer cottage is the ornate **Ochre Court**, the former home of Mr. and Mrs. Ogden Goelet, built in 1888 and now the administration building for Salve Regina University. Next you'll walk past **Cave Cliff**, a pretty wood cottage just past Ochre Court. The curving path soon comes upon **Vinland**, a brownstone Queen Anne villa built in 1883. These are now the grounds of Salve Regina University. The vast lawn is a good place to rest and enjoy the view.

Next, Shepard Avenue joins Cliff Walk. From here, you can look over to Sachuest Beach, Sachuest Point and way out to Sakonnet Light at the tip of Little Compton. Follow the path through the iron gate, and you'll soon notice **The Breakers** looming on the right. There are a few good places to look through the fence for a view of this spectacular mansion. This section is also a favorite place for surfing, as hefty waves continually crash against the rocks. Ruggles Avenue, the road just after The Breakers, is a good place to leave Cliff Walk if you don't wish to do the entire length. At this time you can either explore Ochre Point or walk to Bellevue Avenue for more sightseeing.

If you decide to continue, follow the concrete sidewalk down the incline to surf level, and proceed to where the path turns sharply to the right (west). This is Ochre Point. **Angelsea** (c. 1880) is the rambling stick-style cottage sitting on the point with a commanding view of the ocean. The large Tudor villa next door is **Fairholme** (1870) followed by **Midcliff** (1886) and **Honeysuckle Lodge** (1886).

Looking from the Breakers to Rough Point

Continue around Ochre Point, and you can look across the cove to Beechwood, Rosecliff and Marble House. The Doris Duke mansion, Rough Point, is last on your line of sight. You'll soon notice a small beach where Marine Avenue (dirt road) joins the walk. This is your last opportunity to leave the walk before the end. You can follow Marine Avenue to Bellevue Avenue. The large mansion to the right of Marine Avenue is **Seaview Terrace**.

The remainder of the walk is fascinating, with winding gravel paths and a few short tunnels. However, there are some precarious places where the path all but disappears, and you'll find yourself rock climbing. Near the end, the path improves again.

Most of the mansions you'll see in this area border Bellevue Avenue and can also be viewed from street-side. Walk by a few newer homes, and you'll soon come to **Rosecliff**, the former summer home of Tessie and Birdie Oelrichs and the setting for the movie, "The Great Gatsby". Go up the steps and then look for **Beechwood** beyond the bushes a couple of houses down. Mrs. Caroline Astor, the *grande dame* of Newport society presided royally from Beechwood for many Gilded Age summers. Next, mansion row continues with Alva and William Vanderbilt's stunning **Marble House**. You'll soon walk through a tunnel beneath their recently restored **Chinese Teahouse**. Before entering the tunnel, look back for a great view of the mansions of Ochre Point. **Beaulieu** mansion is on the right, after the tunnel.

At this point, the path descends to near the shoreline and takes a southeast turn to Sheep Point and another tunnel. From this spot, you can probably see more mansions than anywhere in Newport.

Fairholme

Rough Point

Lands End

Look northward to see Ochre Point in the distance and the Bellevue Avenue mansions on the left. For the next half-mile or so, several Bellevue Avenue mansions are above and out of view unless you climb the cliffs (not recommended). Passing unnoticed are **Clarendon Court**, **Miramar** and **Ocean View**. These are described in the Bellevue Avenue tour. The view along this section consists mostly of rock formations, sea birds and surging surf.

Eventually you'll rock climb up to **Rough Point**, the setting for recluse tobacco heiress Doris Duke's gothic mansion of the same name. You'll get a better view of the mansion from here than Bellevue Avenue. Look for camels or other oddities that are sometimes seen roaming the grounds. You may also see a security guard leading a pack of dogs. This 1890 sandstone Tudor mansion, with its great Gothic hall and vast lawns, was once the home of the immensely wealthy financier, Frederick Vanderbilt. Later in the Gilded Age, Mr. and Mrs. William Leeds lived here. The *nouveau riche* Leedes held many lavish balls at Rough Point.

After Rough Point, the Walk works its way gradually westward and is once again high above the sea. You'll have to be very careful here as the rocky path is mostly indistinguishable. The view is spectacular as the ocean roils against the rocks.

Continue another quarter-mile or so, and you'll come to **Land's End**, the former home of Gilded Age novelist and Newport intellectual, Edith Wharton. This three-story, sixteen room stuccoed cottage was built in 1890. At the southern most point of Cliff Walk at Ledge Road, you'll find **The Waves** (c. 1927). This windswept, rambling multi-gabled villa was the home of architect John Russell Pope, designer of the Jefferson Memorial.

The Walk practically ends here, but you could choose to continue along a shoreline path to Bailey's Beach a short distance away, or you can follow Ledge Road to Bellevue Avenue. Senator Claiborne Pell's home is to the left of Ledge Road overlooking the ocean.

The Waves

OCEAN DRIVE

HIGHLIGHTS - The scenery, namely the surf, the rocks and the fabulous houses are highlights of this tour. Hammersmith Farm is open for public touring, and Brenton Park and Fort Adams are state parks open year round.

The route commonly known as Ocean Drive is about eight miles long and consists of several roads, starting with Ocean Avenue at the south end and ending with Wellington Avenue along the Newport waterfront. The route winds along the rocky convoluted coast of southern Aquidneck Island, passing great stone cottages, some perched precariously on the rocks overlooking the Atlantic. Ocean Drive offers explorers a variety of experiences depending upon the weather: the sun glistening off an ocean full of sailing ships, some with spinnakers flying; or the fog forming an eerie mist over the turbulent surf, surging and spraying around the rocks. As you drive along the rugged coastline, notice the abundant birdlife in the inland ponds and ocean coves. In the fall, huge flocks of geese and ducks assemble here to plan their trip south. To appreciate the experience fully, go slowly. Bicycling is a pleasant way, but watch out for cars on the windy road.

Begin your tour at **Bailey's Beach**, the most exclusive of all Gilded Age clubs. This tiny, rather simple looking beach, formally known as the Spouting Rock Beach Association, counted among its members all of the leading families of American society: Astors, Vanderbilts, Belmonts, Goelets, etc., etc. With only eighty-one outside cabanas, it was truly a closed institution.

William Miller built the French chateau sitting on the opposite side of the Bailey's Beach, high above the shore. The stucco and timber facade has the look of a fortress against a hostile environment. Miller appropriately named his house **High Tide** (1900). Automobile baron, Joseph Frazer later owned the mansion.

On the left, just past Bailey's Beach, is a stick-style cottage known as **The Ledges**. This rambling house, built in 1867 for Robert Cushing, has a commanding view of the ocean and the surrounding shoreline. The main house is better viewed from the other side of the point.

Turn right, and go up the hill to Mrs. Stuyvesant Fish's colonial mansion, **Crossways** (1898). Crossways was the scene of many famous social events, several achieving nationwide notoriety and condemnation for their ostentation and decadence. As a member of Newport's Great Triumvirate, the outrageous Mamie Fish was one of the most colorful socialites of the Gilded Age.

The top of this hill is a good place to stop and enjoy the view. As you go down the hill, you'll see **Gooseberry Beach** on the left and **Lily Pond** on the right. Gooseberry Beach is privately owned but open to the public. It offers a great view and swimming in a protected cove (good for young children). Next is **Hazard's Beach**, a private club.

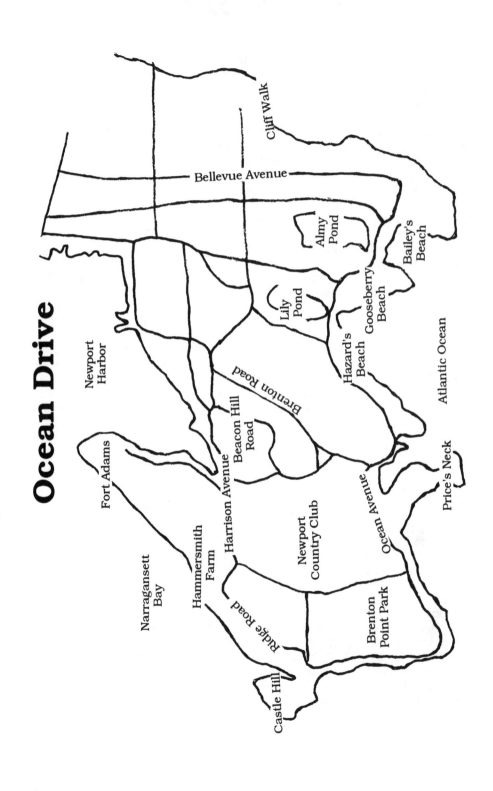

Ocean Drive

Cliff Walk

Bellevue Avenue

Almy Pond

Bailey's Beach

Lily Pond

Gooseberry Beach

Hazard's Beach

Atlantic Ocean

Newport Harbor

Brenton Road

Beacon Hill Road

Fort Adams

Price's Neck

Harrison Avenue

Ocean Avenue

Newport Country Club

Hammersmith Farm

Narragansett Bay

Ridge Road

Brenton Point Park

Castle Hill

High TIde

Crossways

Castle Hill House

Idle Hour is on a hill just west of the Lily Pond. This was the home of Colonel and Mrs. Frederick Allen, who in 1931 hosted French Marshal Henri Petain. Petain, a World War I hero and later Vichyite appeaser, came to Newport aboard a French cruiser to celebrate the 151st anniversary of the French troop landing in Newport. Idle Hour was later owned by Mrs. John Payson Adams, the former Muriel Vanderbilt.

After Hazard's Beach, the road curves to the left and continues to wind past a series of magnificent oceanside cottages: **Nearsea** (1937), **Little Clifton Berley** (1930), **Eagle's Nest** (1924), **Normandie** (1914), **Seafair** (1937), **Bay House** (1917), **Play House** (1926) and **Wildacre** (1901). French and English architectural styles dominate this charming array of houses. Normandie is the brick mansion behind the white wall with an arched gatehouse entrance. Frederick Sterling, a United States Ambassador to Sweden was a former owner. Seafair is an imposing stone mansion sitting on the tip of Cherry Neck. The area just past the Seafair entrance is called **Green End Bridge**, and it's a good place to pull over and enjoy the view (it's also a popular diving and fishing spot). Wildacre was the home of Albert Olmsted. Notice the beautiful landscaping, the Olmsted brothers designed New York's Central Park and were the premier landscape architects of the Gilded Age. At Wildacre, you'll notice Brenton Road on the right, but continue along the ocean road, and look for a small stone projection on the right. It's dotted with rocks and sounds like gushing water when gravel is generously sprinkled over it (try it).

Wrentham House (1891) is past Wildacre, up on a bluff. This secluded stone and shingle mansion was designed by Richard Morris Hunt to blend harmoniously with the surrounding rocks and shrubbery. It's now called Avalon and was recently the home of tennis pioneer James Van Alen. Next you'll come to **Price's Neck**, another popular fishing spot. Here the scene really expands to reveal a wide-open ocean view.

Just after Price's Neck, look for the venerable **Newport Country Club** (1894) on the right. If you want to take a side trip and visit the club, the site of the first U.S. Open, turn at Harrison Avenue and go down about a half-mile to the entrance.

Brenton Point State Park is next, where the road turns north. The park is an excellent place to stop and picnic or just view the scenery. Kite flying is popular in the park, and you'll see all sorts of shapes and styles. You can explore the tidal pools with their variety of sea life, surf fish from the rocks or just watch the great sailing ships as they continually move into and out of the East Passage of Narragansett Bay. For more than fifty years, the America's Cup races were held off of Brenton Point. Once in a while you may still glimpse the sleek Twelve-Meter yachts, unmistakable with their huge sails.

Shortly after you exit the park, turn left at the first road. This road will take you down to the **Castle Hill House** (now The Inn at Castle Hill). In the late 19th century, renowned marine scientist and Harvard professor, Alexander Agassiz lived in this beautiful shingle mansion (1874). The view from this spot is breathtaking with the East Passage at your feet, Jamestown and the Newport Bridge in the background and the charming Castle Hill Light nestled on the shoreline.

Go back to the main road and turn left. Follow the drive a short distance to where it turns left and becomes Ridge Road. You pass the **Coast Guard Station** on the left and Oceancliff (formerly **Shamrock Cliff**) also on the left. Shamrock Cliff (1896) was the G.M. Hutton estate. The main house is patterned after an Irish country castle.

Soon you'll take a sharp right turn and then bear left onto Harrison Avenue. Look for **Hammersmith Farm** looming high on the left. In 1888, John Auchincloss built this twenty-eight room Victorian summer cottage. When John F. Kennedy married Mrs. Hugh Auchincloss' daughter Jacqueline, the wedding reception was held at Hammersmith Farm. Later, President Kennedy made Hammersmith Farm a summer White House.

The shingle-style construction and the airy rooms are appropriate for this seaside cottage. The shingles wear well in the salty air flowing freely through the spacious rooms and terraces. The large deck room is lined with glass doors that open onto a flowered terrace. The grounds and gardens are beautiful, containing a wide variety of trees, shrubs and flowers. A corridor of meticulously pruned silver linden trees is one of the highlights. Various farm animals populate Hammersmith, including a fascinating herd of miniature ponies. Hammersmith Farm is privately owned but open for public touring.

Continue heading back toward Newport on Harrison Avenue, and just after the Hammersmith Farm entrance look for a small farmhouse on the right. This farm was the setting for Harriet Beecher Stowe's novel, "The Minister's Wooing." It was also the home of Janet Auchincloss (Jackie's mother), until she died in 1989.

Turn left into **Fort Adams State Park**. This historic park offers all sorts fascinating diversions including fishing, sailing, swimming and exploring. As you drive down the entrance road, look for a small beach and sailing complex on the right. This is Brenton Cove, summer home to a multitude of sailboats. Look across the cove and you'll see **Beacon Rock** (1889), a classic Georgian mansion perched precariously on the rocks. This Greek temple look-alike was designed by McKim, Mead and White for Edwin Morgan. It was also owned by scientist, Marion Eppley and Felix deWeldon, sculptor of the Iwo Jima statue. Note the Romanesque bridge leading to the mansion.

Continue north toward Fort Adams, and you'll see Newport harbor and skyline appear on the right. You can fish or picnic along the rocks and piers in this area. The Block Island ferry stops here during the summer.

Park in this area and explore the grounds. With Fort Adams on your left and the harbor on the right, follow the paved path out toward the point and the large marker buoy. You can visit the **Museum of Yachting**, the home of the graceful America's Cup J-Boat from 1930, Shamrock V. In addition, the museum has a wealth of yachting memorabilia and exhibits.

You can walk in front of the fort around the point and relax along the rocks to watch a dazzling array of sailing vessels pass before your

Shamrock Cliff

Hammersmith Farm

Beacon Rock

eyes. Every summer the world's best jazz musicians perform at the Newport Jazz Festival held in the broad field in front of the fort.

At its peak, **Fort Adams** was the second largest bastioned fort in the United States, holding a wartime garrison of 2,400 troops and 468 canons. This area was originally fortified in 1776 and later in 1799, when it was named after President John Adams. After the War of 1812, an exposed a weakness in United States coastal defenses led to the construction of a new Fort Adams, beginning in 1824 and ending twenty-three years later. The preeminent military engineer, Colonel Joseph Totten supervised the work. The huge granite blocks used in construction, each weighing several tons, were hauled by schooner, one or two at a time, from northern New England.

The rather mundane look of the external fort belies a complex and intricate web underlying the surface. Complex defenses made Fort Adams practically impenetrable to conventional land assault. Patterned in a classic French style, the geometry of the walls provides an attacker no place to hide without being exposed to a defender's rifle inside the fort.

Deep hidden gullies become shooting galleries when unsuspecting invaders drop between two firewalls full of musketmen. The rocks were designed to ricochet bullets through the attackers. Special listening tunnels penetrate under the fortifications, allowing defenders to hear enemy digging.

The hard cold granite testifies to the harsh life of the garrison, where pneumonia was the greatest enemy. The fort never reached its full occupancy and closed in 1945. Ironically and incredibly, the massive walls were obsolete shortly after construction. The rifled cannon, invented during the Civil War, could powder the once-impregnable walls.

If you like, take the long walk circling the fort, or go directly back to the parking lot. On the way out, notice on the right, the old Victorian mansions now restored as navy housing. Also, look up on the hill near the exit for the **Eisenhower House**, a stately Victorian built in 1873 for the fort commandant and used by President Eisenhower as a summer White House.

Turn left onto Harrison Avenue, go about a half-mile, and look for **Edgehill** on the right. This turreted stone and slate villa is another McKim, Mead and White design, built in 1887 for George King. Edgehill is now a substance abuse treatment center.

At the Edgehill intersection, Harrison Avenue ("the drive") turns left, but instead of turning, you can take an interesting side trip to the interior of the "foot" formed by the lower part of Aquidneck Island. Continue straight (this is Wickham Road), and just after Edgehill, take a sharp right turn onto Beacon Hill Road. This area contrasts greatly with most other parts of Newport. The interior section is pastoral with an abundance of wildlife, rolling meadows, rocky hills and great stone mansions. There's a quiet stillness not found at the coastline just a short distance away. Drive around the circle formed by Beacon Hill Road and Brenton Road, and you'll end up back on Harrison Avenue just a few meters from where you departed.

Remember to keep bearing left as you drive this route, or you'll end up back at the ocean.

Beacon Hill House, the former Arthur Curtiss James residence, is located between Beacon Hill Road and Brenton Road. You can view the house (now named Wyndam) from Beacon Hill Road, it's across from the Edgehill complex. You'll see it again from Brenton Road after passing Cluny School. If you look to the left, you'll notice part of this vast hillside complex. The James estate also contained a Swiss Village. James was a railroad baron who replicated a Swiss farming village in early 20th-century Newport. The original village was complete with stone houses and stables, prize livestock, farm scenes described in verse and a twisting Alpine road cutting through the rocky hills. The village is just past Edgehill, behind the wall.

After you complete the circuit and loop back to Wickham Road, turn left and go back to the junction with Harrison Avenue and Edgehill. Turn right on Harrison Avenue and proceed down to **Beachbound**, where the road turns sharply right. Beachbound (1895) is a huge granite and shingle castle designed by Peabody and Stearns for William Burden. The mansion is on the edge of the water with a great view of Newport harbor.

After the sharp right turn, you'll pass by **Bonniecrest** (1912-1918) on the left. Bonniecrest is a classic Tudor stone and brick manor house designed by John Russell Pope for Stuart Duncan. The Olmsted brothers did the landscaping. Ironically, Bonniecrest resembles country manors in Worcestershire, England, and Mr. Duncan was chairman of Lea and Perrins, makers of Worcestershire Sauce.

After Bonniecrest, turn left on Halidon Avenue and go down the hill to Wellington Avenue and the waterfront. On the left, before the harbor and behind a stone wall, is **Harbour Court**, the former residence of Mrs. John Nicholas Brown of that well-known Providence family. Harbour Court (1904) is an enormous French chateau with a great view of Newport harbor. The New York Yacht Club is the current owner.

This concludes the Ocean Drive tour. You can follow Wellington Avenue back to the Newport waterfront.

Habour Court

WATERFRONT

The popular waterfront stretches south from Goat Island along Long Wharf, down America's Cup avenue, down lower Thames Street, then west on Wellington Avenue to the Ida Lewis Yacht Club.

HIGHLIGHTS - Historic wharves, fascinating shops and restaurants and stunning yachts and sailboats are some of the highlights on this tour.

Begin this tour at **Goat Island**, just west of the Gateway Center. Goat Island is the former sight of a U.S. Navy torpedo station, which saw significant activity during both world wars. Now the island is dominated by a luxury hotel (the **Newport Islander Doubletree Hotel**), a cluster of condominiums and a marina. You can roam the docks and view some hard-to-believe yachts that could be mistaken for ocean liners. Goat Island is reached from a causeway connected to the mainland at Washington Street.

After crossing the causeway, walk south along Washington street, and you'll come to the **State Pier**, the location of a sizable fishing fleet. Turn left on Long Wharf and follow the road to the east. On the right you'll see the **Newport Yacht Club**, and the **Newport Marriott Hotel** is on the left. Long Wharf continues across America's Cup Avenue (but you might not realize it because the street becomes a pedestrian mall). In this area you'll find the **Brick Marketplace**, a complex of stores situated between America's Cup Avenue and Thames Street.

Back at the corner of America's Cup Avenue and Long Wharf, **Perotti Park** offers a panoramic view of the harbor and a place to rest. Continue south on America's Cup Avenue past the **Newport Harbor Hotel & Marina**, and you'll find the shopping complex of **Bowen's Wharf** and **Bannister's Wharf**. This area, like the Brick Marketplace, contains all sorts of innovative and interesting shops and restaurants. Peter Harrison and his wife owned this wharf in colonial times, They lived in a big house on Thames Street at the head of the wharf. George Bowen bought the wharf in 1831 and provided parts and services to Newport's large sailing fleet. Many of the old structures remain. Several sumptuous yachts dock along these wharves.

Sayer's Wharf is next as you walk south. It's the former home of the New York Yacht Club (now the Mooring Restaurant). Continue south, past the **Newport Yachting Center** on the right, to where America's Cup Avenue meets Thames Street. The **Perry Mill** (now the Newport Bay Club) is at the corner. This historic granite structure was built in 1835 by Alexander McGregor and was originally a textile mill. Proceed down lower Thames street. The vast array of shops, restaurants and inns continues on both sides of the street. As you go along, explore the various wharves extending from Thames street to the waterfront.

81

Waterfront

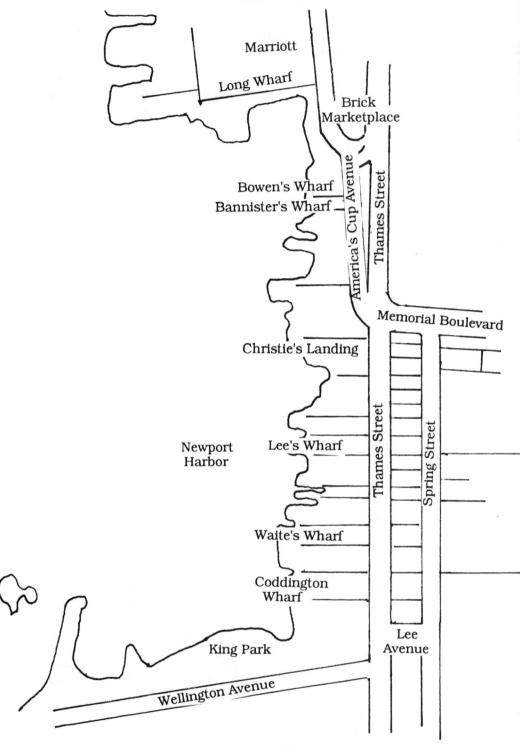

Marriott

Long Wharf

Brick
Marketplace

Bowen's Wharf

Bannister's Wharf

America's Cup Avenue

Thames Street

Memorial Boulevard

Christie's Landing

Newport
Harbor

Lee's Wharf

Thames Street

Spring Street

Waite's Wharf

Coddington
Wharf

Lee
Avenue

King Park

Wellington Avenue

Bannister's Wharf

You'll find a treasure trove of interesting discoveries. At **Christies' Landing** (one block south of Perry Mill), you'll find a popular outdoor watering hole and an variety of incredible yachts. Walk down the **Ann Street Pier** (just past the Inn on the Harbor) for a good view of the waterfront.

There are several notable houses along this section of Thames Street. Francis Malbone, a colonial merchant prince, lived in the imposing three-story brick mansion at 392 Thames Street. The **Malbone House** (c. 1758) demonstrates the great wealth of Newport's colonial merchants. Malbone was heavily involved in the triangle trade, and locating his house near the waterfront was no coincidence. Evidence indicates a basement tunnel used for smuggling goods past the watchful eye of the King's customs agents. Note the tiny counting house next to the mansion.

Merchant **Clarke Burdick** built his house at 413 Thames Street. Built in 1835, this house shows Greek Revival details. Note the sidelights in the doorway. The **James Record House** (c. 1835) is next door at 415 Thames Street. This Greek Revival, with another nice doorway is set end to the street.

Across the street, on the corner with Dennison Street, you'll find the **Samuel Whitehorne House**, a fine example of Federal period (1783-1815) architecture. Captain Samuel Whitehorne, Jr. built this house

Christie's Landing

James House

in 1811. Whitehorne was another wealthy triangle-trade shipping merchant who owned several businesses. The loss of two ships led to bankruptcy, and in 1844 the house was sold at auction. The brick exterior is simple and symmetrical. A circular cyclopean window and a rounded portico dominate the centerline, in sharp contrast to the block-like solidity exhibited by the rest of the exterior. The interior is resplendent with 18th-century Goddard and Townsend furniture, works of Newport silversmiths and pewterers, oriental rugs and Chinese porcelain. The floor plan consists of a central hall surrounded by four rooms on each floor with four chimneys extending along the exterior walls. **Brown and Howard Wharf** (at Dennison Street) is another interesting wharf to walk down and explore.

The **James Boone House**, c. 1798, is at 422 Thames Street. Boone was a ship's carpenter. He built this gable roofed house with a fine fanlight doorway. The **Hunter-Whitehorne House** at 428 Thames Street was built in 1750. This shallow hip-roofed house has noteworthy interior details like original paneling, an elaborate stairway and finely detailed mantles. The house and an adjoining distillery were bought by Samuel Whitehorne in 1794. This house is at the corner with Young Street.

Continue along Thames Street past several explorable wharves: **Lee's, Spring, Waite's and Coddington.**

You'll soon come to Wellington Avenue (just past the Wellington condominiums). Turn right on Wellington Avenue, and walk along the sidewalk to **King Park**. This tiny park includes a small beach and offers a great view of Newport's harbor and skyline. Look for the statue of French General Rochambeau pointing toward victory at Yorktown as his army left Newport from this very spot.

As you continue along Wellington Avenue, you're treated to a great view of assorted boats scurrying about the harbor. The venerable **Ida Lewis Yacht Club** is near the end of Wellington Avenue and marks the end of the downtown waterfront. Precariously perched on Lime Rock, the Ida Lewis Yacht Club is a prominent landmark in Newport harbor. The club is named for Idawalley Zorada Lewis, the keeper of the Lime Rock lighthouse during the late 19th-century. Ida Lewis was the heroine in several sea rescues, and in 1881 she received a Congressional medal for heroism. Now the yacht club has replaced the lighthouse and is a popular location for sailing activities.

Double back on Wellington Avenue to Thames Street, and follow Lee Avenue up the hill to Spring Street. Turn left on Spring Street and walk north, back towards Memorial Boulevard.

The **James House** is on the corner of Spring Street and Lee Avenue. Renowned novelist Henry James and famed philosopher/psychologist William James lived in this large three-story stone house. The James brothers lived here during their formative years from 1861 to 1864. Henry James wrote with fondness about his time in Newport. He read in Redwood Library and went on long walks with stained-glass artist John La Farge and other friends. It was La Farge's influence that spawned Henry's writing career. The vast estate across the street is The Elms (see Bellevue Avenue tour).

Exploring this section of Spring Street, you'll note good sample of 18th and 19th century buildings.

Continue along Spring Street to Bowery Street. **Aquidneck Park**, the location of the Newport Public Library, is between Bowery Street and Golden Hill Street. The **Edward King House**, c. 1847, is at the top of Aquidneck Park. This Italianate villa designed by Richard Upjohn, has a massive asymmetrical exterior featuring smooth brick walls, projecting roofs, loggias, balconies and Italianate trim. A pivotal central hall dominates the interior. The King House is a National Historic Landmark and is now used as a senior citizens center.

Turn right at Golden Hill Street and walk up the hill, past the **Nathaniel Gladding House** (c.1771) and the **William Gyles House** (c.1773) to the **Clifton Burial Ground**. Explore this tiny cemetery, and you'll find a treasure of early 18th century graves, including those of four colonial governors: Walter and Jeremy Clarke and Joseph and William Wanton.

Follow the road around to the left and go back down the hill on William Street. On the way down, look for the diminutive **Benjamin Hammett House** (c. 1790) on the left.

Turn right at Spring Street, and walk in front of **Saint Mary's Roman Catholic Church**. This beautiful English Gothic style church was built between 1848 and 1852 and is the oldest Catholic parish (1828) in Rhode Island. This church is famous as the place where, on September 12, 1953, John Kennedy married Jacqueline Bouvier of Hammersmith Farm. It's now a National Historic Shrine.

Turn left, and go down Memorial Boulevard to America's Cup Avenue. From here you can follow America's Cup Avenue back to the Gateway Center.

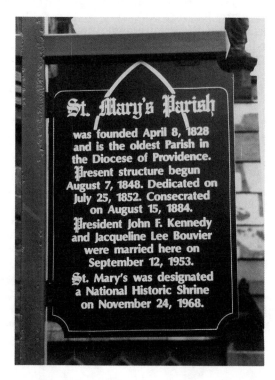

RECOMMENDED RESTAURANTS

Restaurants are among Newport's finest assets; they are numerous and cover a broad range of taste. The sea is Newport's forte, and seafood is special. Freshness is assured: Newport is a leading New England fishing port.

The ambiance compliments the food to make dining in Newport a sensual experience. Newport dining is also a diverse experience. You may dine in colonial charm exuded by a restored historic building, experience the soothing sophistication of an elegant wharf bistro, watch a continual parade of sailboats while having brunch on a patio, view the sunset over the harbor from the deck of a waterfront restaurant, enjoy the conviviality in a lively pub or relax in an intimate cafe.

In addition to the usually reliable prime rib, filet mignon, lobster (especially good), sole, schrod, scallops, clams and shrimp, you may encounter all sorts of special treats unique to each restaurant. Items particularly indigenous to the Newport area are swordfish, bluefish, lobster, mussels (Narragansett Bay), clam chowder, hard-shell clams called quahogs ("co-hogs"), steamed clams, a spicy Portuguese sausage known as Chourico (Sher-eese), and jonnycakes (cornmeal pancakes). Rhode Islanders also love coffee syrup (Eclipse or Autocrat). They often eat French fries with vinegar and eggs with ketchup. Submarine sandwiches are often called grinders, milk shakes are called frappes (or cabinets), and soda is sometimes called tonic (although rarely anymore).

The restaurants listed below are recommended by the author based on a variety of information including personal opinion. Undoubtedly there are other fine restaurants which are not included simply because they are either new or there is just insufficient information. The author would appreciate any opinions you have regarding Newport's restaurants. Most of the restaurants are in or around the waterfront area, close to hotels and inns. So walk if you can.

Pubs

The Brick Alley Pub
"Meticulous attention to detail"

140 Thames Street - To find the Brick Alley Pub, look for the yellow and white striped awnings over tall store-front windows in the old Newport Daily News building across from the Brick Marketplace. The Brick Alley Pub is extremely popular and pulsates with activity all season long. Restaurateurs Ralph and Pat Plumb have decorated the

interior with fascinating memorabilia and artifacts from their travels throughout the United States and Mexico. Local fresh seafood and southwestern specialties highlight an extensive and diverse menu, which includes house specialties like Sole Vanderbilt (stuffed with scallops, crabs, mushrooms and cheese) and a broad variety of burgers, special sandwiches, dinner and luncheon entrees, appetizers, soups, salads and lobsters. Other house specialties include nachos, fajitas, Irish Coffee and strawberry daiquiris. The Brick Alley Pub is a fun place with a menu that won't quit. **Notes**: Sunday brunch, outdoor courtyard, game room, credit cards, prices from $4.95-$19.95. **Trivia**: sixth busiest restaurant in R.I. (busiest per seat). Phone 849-6334.

Yesterday's
"The place where Newporters go."

28 Washington Square - Yesterday's is located in the heart of colonial Newport and bustles with activity year round. Newporters flock to Yesterday's to enjoy the expansive menu and leisurely ambiance of this convivial saloon/restaurant. The interior is reminiscent of a Victorian club, with stained glass, tin ceiling, antique Tiffany lamps, tapestries, hanging plants, dark woods and old-time pictures. The large mahogany bar in the middle of the dining room is a great place to "people watch".

You can get a wide variety of salads, soups, burgers and specialty sandwiches. There's also a good Mexican selection featuring Mexican pizza. A blackboard jammed with daily specials may include broiled swordfish, baked trout with almonds and pineapple or roast duck.

A new wine bar and grille adjoins the pub through an archway. This innovative restaurant features gourmet entrees and all sorts of wines by the glass. **Notes**: credit cards, limited parking. Phone 847-0116.

The Ark
"Great location, beautiful decor, lots of fun."

348 Thames Street - Strategically located at the busy junction of Thames Street and Memorial Boulevard, the British-owned Ark is a large black building with lots of windows. This classic building, constructed in 1898, is listed on the National Register of Historic Places. The ground floor is an authentic English-style pub serving all sorts of creative sandwiches, appetizers, salads and entrees. Upstairs, you'll find a wonderful dining room romantically decorated in apricot, muted green and gray. Stenciled walls, marbleized wood, Oriental carpeting, potted plants and draped windows complete the scene.

The dining room menu is mostly American with international influences. Typical offerings may include blackened catfish with garlic flavored mayonnaise, roast duck breast with fig and pecan sauce or "Steak of the Ark", served with green peppercorns, mustard, shallots and a brandy cream sauce. **Notes**: credit cards, Sunday brunch, no parking, breakfast (summer). **Trivia**: Prince Andrew ate here during the 1983 America's Cup. Phone 849-3808.

Marina Pub
"Quaint and salty."

Goat Island- Quaint and salty, the Marina Pub sits in the midst of yacht country in the Goat Island Marina. In the summertime, many of the patrons come from the surrounding yachts to enjoy the casual pub atmosphere. The plain decor is occasionally livened by some nautical artifact, but the Marina Pub is not fancy by any means. Blackboard specials abound. The Marina Pub is on Goat Island and offers an excellent panorama of Newport harbor. The menu is varied with all sorts of sandwiches, appetizers and soups. They have a Sunday brunch. **Notes**: Phone 846-2675.

Mudville Pub
"Good crowd, good service, good time"

8 West Marlborough Street - Maybe there was no joy in Mudville when mighty Casey struck out, but there's plenty of joy at the Mudville Pub. Located along the right field line of venerable Cardine's Field, the Mudville is a cozy pub with a sports motif. Dark wood furnishings, television screens and conviviality abound. The Mudville is owned by Former Boston Celtic and Providence College basketball star, Kevin Stacom (you're likely to see him mingling with the customers). Daily specials usually include pasta, fish and chicken; salads, appetizers and sandwiches are plentiful. The hamburgers are highly recommended.
The Mudville Pub is extremely popular with both locals and tourists (it's located less than a block from the Newport Marriott Hotel). In the summertime, you can lounge on the outdoor patio (protected by fencing, top and sides) and watch an exciting baseball game. **Notes**: credit cards. **Trivia**: frequented by Boston sports stars. Phone 849-1408.

Bistros/Cafes

Pronto
"Best pasta in Newport"

464 Thames Street- This romantic storefront bistro will charm you with eclectic Mediterranean ambiance and wonderful food. Fresh flowers, antique chandeliers and potted palms decorate the intimate dining room. The tiny open-air kitchen in the back of the room

specializes in gourmet Italian dishes, all presented with flair. Particularly recommended are the angel hair with black olive and prosciutto sauce and the farfalle (butterfly-shaped pasta) with shiitake mushrooms, calamata olives, roast red peppers, spinach, pignola nuts and chevre cheese. Creative daily specials usually include seafood, steak or fowl, and you may encounter such delights as potato and herb crusted red snapper with yellow pepper vinaigrette or duck with shiitake raviolis and sun-dried tomatoes.

Pronto has an imaginative wine list, with several served by the glass. After dinner, you can enjoy an espresso or cappuccino. There's also a tiny, tiny bar for before or after dinner drinks. **Notes**: credit cards, wine and beer only, breakfast (summer) and lunch, dinner prices from $8 to $15. Phone 847-5251.

The Rhumbline
"Warm, cozy and colonial"

62 Bridge Street - Located in the midst of colonial Newport, The Rhumbline will take you back to an 18th century tavern in the Golden Age of Newport. Meticulously restored houses and gaslit streets surround The Rhumbline and make up the Point section--Newport's oldest. Former offshore fisherman Stephen Giunta has owned The Rhumbline since 1980. The restaurant is frequented by locals, and its warm relaxing atmosphere will give you a flavor of both colonial and contemporary Newport.

Plenty of natural wood and hanging plants welcome you to the warm interior. Check the portable blackboard for daily specials. For an appetizer or a light meal, the mussels are highly recommended. Other light meals are available: hamburgers, sandwiches, soups and salads. Main dishes vary but usually include fish, veal or chicken. Weinerschnitzel, stuffed seafood and curried mussel soup are specialties. You can get fine wine by the glass. **Notes**: Sunday brunch, credit cards, lunch ($4.95-$7.95), dinner ($10.95-$18.95), park at the nearby Bridge Street lot. Phone 849-6950.

Scales and Shells
"See, hear and smell your dinner cooking"

527 Thames Street - Billing itself as Newport's only "fish only" restaurant, Scales and Shells is a fun place to eat from an abundant menu of seafood. Dining is decidedly informal in a large room with an open-air kitchen. Retired sea captain, Andrew Ackerman and his wife Debra, a former teacher are the chef/owners.

You can get clams, shrimp, scallops, blackfish, bluefish, swordfish, monkfish, tunafish, red snapper...... Specialties include Lobster Fra Diavolo, grilled clam pizza, calamari, wood-grilled fish, as well as a selection of southern Italian seafood. **Notes**: no credit cards, checks

OK with ID, beer and wine only, entrees from $9 to $17. Phone 846-FISH.

The International Cafe
"Innovative food, old fashioned prices"

677 Thames Street - Behind a simple plate-glass storefront, you'll find sumptuous international cuisine at bargain-basement prices. Located on "lowest" Thames Street, this little one-story cafe with limited ambiance (you won't care) serves up really good food. If you like stir fry, try the Oriental spaghetti stir fried with shrimp, vegetables and garlic; the Pancit Behon, thin Philippine noodles stir fried with vegetables, garlic and chicken or pork; or shrimp and scallops stir fried with Oriental vegetables. The cosmopolitan menu continues with Scallops Parisienne (mushrooms, white wine and cheddar cheese), Polynesian fried shrimp (sweet and sour sauce) and Szechuan steak or lobster. All entrees come in two sizes, depending on your appetite. **Notes**: BYOB, credit cards, some parking on street, entrees from $6 to $12. Phone 847-1033.

Pezzuli's
"Italy on Thames"

136 Thames Street - Pezzulli's overlooks the Brick Marketplace from its second-story perch next to the Brick Alley Pub. Pavarotti posters and Italian flags decorate the small L-shaped dining room. Chef/owner Barbara Pezzulli creates an imaginative array of authentic Italian regional and peasant dishes. For an appetizer, try the grilled Italian bread with tomatoes and basil. If you like lobster, you just might love the Aragosta Fra Diavolo, lots of lobster meat served in a spicy marinara sauce over black squid ink pasta. The Rotelle col Sugo di Salsicce is a cartwheel pasta served al dente with spicy Italian sausage in a creamy tomato sauce. And for dessert, there's Tirami Su, a cake-like concoction made with Italian lady fingers, espresso, rum, mascarpone cheese and chocolate dust.
Notes: no credit cards, BYOB, entrees $8 and up, dinner includes salad and freshly baked loaf of bread, Italian brunch Sat/Sun. Phone 846-5830.

Puerini's
"Casual"

24 Memorial Boulevard - The Puerini family dishes out delicious Italian food at a rather frenetic pace. Puerini's is as unpretentious and informal as they come. Crowds abound for most of the year, and you may find yourself waiting outside. Although the quarters can be tight, the casual dining and friendly service are enjoyable. Italian

treats include cavatelli baked in four cheeses, topped with red and yellow peppers and onions or filet of sole stuffed with seafood, cheese and spinach, served with green noodles in a garlicky red sauce. **Notes**: no credit cards, BYOB, no smoking, dinner for two ranges between $20 and $30. **Trivia**: proclaimed the state's best pasta by RI Monthly magazine. Phone 847-5506.

Le Bistro
"A light touch of France"

Bowen's Wharf - Wood beams and open stairways are prominent in the modern multi-level interior of this informal French-style restaurant. Le Bistro is located in an unassuming clapboard building in the highly popular Bowen's Wharf complex.

Chef/owner John Philcox looks for interesting and uncommon ways to use fresh local products in his cuisine, which he describes as "modern French." He uses light sauces meant to enhance rather than overwhelm the natural flavors of his ingredients. The ever-changing menu could include such items as scallops with beets in pastry, sirloin brochette with vegetable stir fry or veal kidneys in a mustard and brandy sauce. For dessert, try Le Bistro's specialty, chocolate walnut cake with brandy butter filling and apricot glaze. There's a wide selection of wine, particularly French; however, Rhode Island wines from the Sakonnet Vineyard are also available.

There's a third-floor bar overlooking the harbor and busy Bowen's Wharf. **Notes**: credit cards, brunch Sat/Sun, limited parking. Phone 849-7778.

Salas'
"Good food at the right price"

341-343 Thames Street - Salas', located at the beginning of lower Thames Street, is the one of the best bargains in town. The food is good, the prices are right, and the service is friendly. The Salas family started this restaurant in 1952 when lower Thames had mostly fishermen and dilapidated honky -tonk bars, no tourists. Judging from the large local following, they run in right. The atmosphere is not intimate, but it is informal. The 19th-century Victorian building was originally a bank and then a general store. Check out the heavy oak staircase and tin ceilings. In the summer, Salas' is nearly always crowded, so arrive early to avoid the line.

Italian food and seafood dominate the menu, and portions are plentiful (spaghetti is sold by weight). Salas' Clambake is everything you'd expect from a traditional New England clambake and more: lobster, clams, fish, sausage, corn-on-the-cob, potato and onion. There's also steak and house specialty, Oriental Spaghetti (linguine made with pork, shrimp or chicken and served with fried rice). **Notes**: credit cards, no parking, raw bar and seafood deli. Phone 846-8772.

Elizabeth's
"Enjoy food by the platter"

Brown and Howard Wharf - Elizabeth's is a charming blend of English living room ambiance and unique culinary style. Proprietor Elizabeth Burley is an Englishwoman recently transplanted from Manhattan to Newport. The homey high-ceilinged interior gives the impression of a farmhouse living room stocked with eclectic antiques (paisley tablecloths, stuffed chairs). Elizabeth serves entrees on huge platters for two, so dine with a compatible partner. You'll marvel at these luscious platters which vary nightly. The barbecue platter is particularly appealing with chicken, spareribs, sweet potato pie, baked beans, apples, roast potato and onions. The accompanying sliced cheese bread is stuffed with zucchini, squash and broccoli. The seafood bouillabaisse is served in a hollowed-out sourdough loaf filled with mussels, shrimp and scallops on a bed of pasta marinara, accompanied by hot sausage and assorted grilled vegetables. You'll love poking through these platters and discovering new delights. **Notes**: BYOB, credit cards, courtyard dining, platters around $40 for two. Phone 846-6862.

Mexican Cafe
"Best bargain in Newport"

150 Broadway - Far from the madding crowd, this absolutely unpretentious cafe serves the best deal in town. The Mexican Cafe is a simple storefront restaurant on commonplace Broadway, a couple of blocks from the police station. The Spartan decor and zero ambiance belie the excellent food. You'll find a broad selection of Mexican and Cajun dishes including; chicken, beef and cheese enchiladas/burritos; fajitas; tacos; Chili Rellano (pepper stuffed with cheese, fried in egg batter and served with ranchero sauce); blackened catfish and swordfish (fresh, grilled on cast-iron and served with jambalaya); Creole chicken; and shrimp pasta (shrimp sautéed with ham, mushrooms, scallions and peppers and tossed with spinach pasta). You'll encounter all sorts of interesting seasonings, marinates and sauces. Most of the Mexican dishes are served with a perfect combination of blackbeans and rice. **Notes**: BYOB (no extra charge), credit cards, entrees range from $5 to $11. Phone 849-4203.

Epicurean

La Petite Auberge
"Paris in Newport"

19 Charles Street- Petite it is (seating only 48), but La Petite Auberge is considered one of the finest French restaurants in New England. La Petite Auberge is located in a classic colonial Newport house near Washington Square. The charming house contains several intimate dining rooms decorated with antique furniture and paintings. Plush curtains and carpeting combine with linen and lace table settings to complete the romantic scene. The decor is muted blue and gray downstairs and soft green and gold upstairs.

Superb sauces complement classic dishes. Beef Wellington (filet mignon) with truffle sauce and lobster tails in champagne sauce are outstanding examples. Escargots with mushroom sauce and duck with raspberries and duck sauce are house specialties. For dessert, you can get crepes Suzette, strawberries Romanoff, cherries jubilee or banana flambe.

Technique and style set La Petite Auberge apart from most restaurants. Skillful service includes waiters and busgirls in tuxedos. La Petite Auberge is an expensive delight for the senses. **Notes**: credit cards, limited parking, courtyard dining. Phone 849-6669.

Canfield House
"Gilded Age elegance"

5 Memorial Boulevard - Richard Canfield, a New Bedford gambler and inventor of Solitaire, established a gambling casino here in 1897. The elegant casino catered to the wealthy elite of Newport's Gilded Age. Canfield also served gourmet meals in his casino, a tradition carried on today by Diane Whitehead, owner of the Canfield House restaurant.

The lavish interior will take you back to turn-of-the-century Newport, with dark paneled walls, stained glass, vaulted twenty-foot ceilings and Victorian furniture. The setting is formal, but the service is gracious and friendly. When you're visiting the Victorian lounge, check out the painting behind the bar, and see how many Canfield employees you can pick out.

The fare is American with a continental touch. The Canfield House is well-known for its Chateaubriand, a succulent Black Angus cut served with béarnaise sauce and fresh vegetables. Veal and seafood (procured daily from Newport's waterfront) frequent the menu, and the large baked stuffed lobster is extremely popular. **Notes**: credit cards, free parking, breakfast (summer). **Trivia**: The Canfield is listed on the National Register of Historic Places. Phone 847-0416.

The Black Pearl
"Classic food, classic location"

Bannister's Wharf - The Black Pearl is nearly a Newport landmark. Situated amidst the bustle of Bannister's Wharf, the Black Pearl is a deluxe French-style restaurant. A simple shingled exterior belies the elegance of this dockside restaurant. The luxurious Commodore Room (main dining room), staffed by tuxedoed waiters, is formally decorated with black walls and white and crystal table settings. The menu includes such delicacies as; shrimp, scallops and lobster with lobster sauce in a puff pastry; veal medallions with champagne sauce; and Black Pearl Rack of Lamb. You may also find grilled entrees like duck breast, pheasant breast or salmon steak.

The salty tavern section offers excellent clam chowder, salads and sandwiches. **Notes**: credit cards, entrees $16 to $26, very limited parking, good wine list. Phone 846-5264.

Inn at Castle Hill
"Unparalleled Victorian ambiance and a view that won't quit"

Ocean Avenue - This imposing mansion majestically overlooks the most spectacular view in Newport. From a prominent peninsula, the Inn at Castle Hill guards the channel connecting the Atlantic Ocean to the East Passage of Narragansett Bay. In the summertime, a continuous parade of sailboats--some with spinnakers flying-- provides a breathtaking view.

Owner Paul McEnroe has preserved the elegant interior of this 19th-century country mansion. Visitors are taken back in time amidst elaborate wood carvings, hand-crafted Victorian wood paneling and all sorts of Oriental and 19th-century artwork. Specialties include reliable fresh salmon, Beef Wellington and other interesting dishes such as duck with peppercorns and brandy sauce and stuffed filet of sole with lobster sauce, mussels, and mushrooms.

A Newport experience is not complete without Sunday brunch in the garden room or on the terrace. The food is good but outclassed by the view. If you're not careful in the summertime, you could spend an entire afternoon (later they barbecue hamburgers and hot-dogs on an outdoor grill) watching a magnificent sunset over Jamestown Island.

Notes: credit cards, brunch, lounge, lodging, expensive, park on the premises. **Trivia**: Home of famed 19th century Harvard marine scientist and inveterate traveler, Alexander Agassiz (see Ocean Drive tour). Phone 849-3800.

The Whitehorse Tavern
"Nice place to impress your date"

Corner of Farewell and Marlborough streets - The Whitehorse Tavern bills itself as "America's oldest eating and drinking establishment". The building is a classic colonial, exhibiting features from both the 17th and 18th centuries. For more information on the building, see the Point East walking tour.

Romantic colonial ambiance will take you back to the Golden Age of Newport, and in the subdued glow of the flickering candles you can almost imagine Newport patriots plotting the American Revolution. The menu offers gourmet continental and American cuisine featuring native seafood dishes, beef, lamb and venison. Customer favorites include Lobster Whitehorse Tavern (a large lobster removed from its shell and sautéed with tomatoes, basil, brandy and cream) and baked Norwegian salmon coated in a crisp potato crust with tomato and lemon grass.

The cozy bar is especially enjoyable for after dinner brandy, and in the wintertime you can warm up by the cavernous fireplace.

Notes: credit cards, private parking lot, entrees range $21- $30, extensive wine list. **Trivia**: you can get a private tour by the Whitehorse's own curator. Phone 849-3600.

La Forge Casino
"Victorian dining on the 'Avenue'"

186 Bellevue Avenue - The La Forge will take you back to the Gilded Age of Newport. Turn-of-Century ambiance abounds in this Victorian restaurant located in the stately Newport Casino. The dining room overlooks the meticulously manicured tennis and croquet lawns of the Casino. New England seafood dishes are special and include; the Old New England Fish Platter with fried shrimp, scallops and fish served with lobster salad; swordfish (try it char-grilled over an open flame); baked stuffed shrimp with lobster stuffing; and Lobster Casino (tails and claws breaded and fried). You can also get Chateaubriand for two, served with garden vegetables, mushrooms, baked potato, béarnaise sauce and a half-liter of wine ($40).

You can dine casually in the front of the restaurant and choose from a varied pub menu of sandwiches, salads, soups and entrees. The adjoining Victorian pub offers soothing atmosphere and occasional entertainment. The La Forge is highly popular with local Newporters. Newport's Crowley family runs the La Forge. The Crowleys trace their roots back to Ireland and offer an original Irish breakfast as part of their Sunday brunch. **Notes**: credit cards, park across the street, entrees range from $14 to $20. **Trivia**: one of the owners, Paul Crowley, is a RI congressman. Phone 847-0418.

Cafe del Mare
"Best hotel restaurant in town"

Newport Marriott Hotel - Yes, there is a gourmet Italian restaurant right inside Newport's largest hotel. You'll have to walk through J.W.'s Seagrill and under an iron-gated arch to this bit of Northern Italy. But you'll find the trek worth it as you choose from a menu featuring such delights as veal chop stuffed with fontina cheese in a Madeira wine sauce, artichoke-stuffed ravioli with prosciutto, Penne Cafe del Mare (pasta with cream, bacon and Parmesan) or veal rolled with prosciutto and mozzarella in Marsala wine. Try an appetizer like mussels with mozzarella and fresh basil or a salad of arugula, endive, radicchio and beets with raspberry vinaigrette. **Notes**: credit cards, parking, dinner for two $40 to $50. Phone 849-7788.

Cooke House
"Elegance on the wharf"

Bannister's Wharf - The Cooke House is an imposing three-story colonial mansion, the former home of a sea captain. In the early 1970's the house was moved to Bannister's Wharf where it was restored and opened as a restaurant. Extremely popular Bannister's Wharf is jammed in the summertime and is a great place to mingle and enjoy the waterfront.
Elegant place settings of pure white cloth and crystal combine with 18th-century antiques and paintings to reflect an aura of relaxation in the candlelit atmosphere. Old wooden staircases connect multi-level dining rooms, and bare floorboards recall the rustic roots of this colonial masterpiece. The Cooke House has its own farm (Farmlands) in nearby Portsmouth, providing lamb, game and fresh fruit and vegetables to the restaurant every day. The classic French cuisine may include breast of pheasant in cider sauce, roast rack of lamb with tarragon glaze (a house specialty), Nova Scotia smoked salmon salad or grilled swordfish with buckwheat fettucini.
The service is meticulous and professional. You can have a drink on the deck and enjoy the wharf scenery. **Notes**: credit cards, limited parking, prices are high, Sunday brunch. **Trivia**: the proprietors also own Boston's famed Locke-Ober restaurant. Phone 849-2900.

Smuggler's Landing
"Best harbor view"

Long Wharf - You'll find Smuggler's Landing on the second floor of The Inn at Long Wharf. A glass elevator opens to an ultra-modern interior with plate glass wrapping around two sides of the building. Smuggler's has a panoramic view of the busy harbor. You'll enjoy watching all the activity through the picture windows or from the canopied deck. Prohibition era smugglers plied their trade along Long

Wharf, hence the name Smuggler's Landing. Keeping with this tradition, Smuggler's specializes in "Island" food, particularly Pacific and Caribbean. You may find Hawaiian sweet and sour shrimp, Sri Lankan curried chicken, West Indian jumbo shrimp or Gulf red snapper. House signature dishes include tea-smoked breast of black duck. You can also get Aquidneck Island specialties like grilled native lobster. **Notes**: credit cards, valet parking, week-end entertainment, entrees $12 to $20. Phone 847-7800.

Newport Waterfront Traditional

The Pier
"One of the oldest on the waterfront"

West Howard Wharf - The Pier is just off lower Thames Street in a low but long building sitting at the end of West Howard Wharf amidst the yachts and fishing boats. Barnboard and maritime mementos adorn the simple interior. There's a broad selection of seafood, supplied locally, as well as char-broiled steaks, chops, roast beef and duckling. The chunky fish chowder is particularly recommended as an appetizer. The abundant clambake is a popular entree. For dessert try the voluptuous ice cream pie. There's an outdoor deck for summer relaxation and a lively lounge with entertainment. **Notes**: Amex, parking. Phone 847-3645.

Christie's
"May be the most popular restaurant in town"

Christie's Landing, at the beginning of Lower Thames Street - Christie's is traditional Newport, it's the oldest restaurant on the waterfront. Located in the midst of fabulous yachts, Christie's buzzes with activity all summer. Christie's Landing (outside) has a cocktail deck that's normally crowded with afternoon revelers, and shakes in the evening with a contemporary band. The restaurant is huge with two levels and a spacious barroom. The walls are dotted with pictures of America's Cup yachts and famous people who have visited the restaurant. Celebrities frequent Christie's.
Seafood is popular, particularly lobster. The food is good, but not outstanding. Christie's is special because it's the place to go for fun, entertainment and traditional New England food. **Notes**: credit cards, parking lot (usually full in season), entrees priced medium to high. **Trivia**: Billy Joel and Christie Brinkley come here. Phone 847-5400.

The Mooring
"Watch the yachts"

<u>Sayer's Wharf, next to Bannister's Wharf</u> - Formerly occupied by the New York Yacht Club, this classic building is now a waterfront restaurant. The Mooring has retained much of the yacht club charm, with a massive fireplace, open-air deck and walls decked with pictures of old Newport completing the scene. The Mooring is a great location to enjoy the waterfront; large picture windows provide a panoramic view of the harbor with Goat Island and Jamestown in the background.

The Mooring features lobster, shrimp, scallops, crab legs, steak and prime rib. There's a varied selection of house wines (some by the glass) and an extensive beer list. **Notes**: credit cards, pay to park, entrees from $14 to $21. Phone 846-2260.

The Ark

LODGINGS

Newport has a wide variety of hotels, inns, guest houses and bed and breakfast establishments. Hotel rooms in Newport are generally expensive ($125 to $250 per night in the summer). Guest houses and small inns are less expensive and offer local color and Newport ambiance. In a guest house you may share a bath, but you'll also have a chance to mingle with other guests and proprietors who usually offer a wealth of Newport knowledge. Most guest houses serve a continental breakfast, and many offer a common sitting room for guests. Prices for all accommodations are much less in the late fall, winter and early spring. There's a 12% sales tax on all rooms in Newport.

During the summer rooms go fast, so try to reserve at least a month ahead. At guest houses, a deposit and a two-night minimum stay (on week-ends) may be required.

Hotels

The **Newport Marriott Hotel** is situated in the heart of the city on America's Cup Avenue and Long Wharf. The Marriott is Newport's largest hotel with 317 rooms. The usual Marriott amenities are here. Relax and have a drink in the spacious atrium or enjoy the harbor view from the Oyster Bar. Dine at the Cafe del Mare or dance in Tickets lounge. First class and beautiful. 849-1000.

The **Newport Islander Doubletree Hotel** is on Goat Island in the middle of Newport harbor. This 250-room hotel offers a spectacular view of both Narragansett Bay and the Newport waterfront. The entire hotel has been recently renovated. Looks good. 849-2600.

The **Newport Harbor Hotel and Marina** is ideally located on the waterfront along America's Cup Avenue. It's in the midst of popular Bowen's and Bannister's wharves. 134 rooms. 847-9000.

The stately **Viking Hotel** sits atop Historic Hill at One Bellevue Avenue. This historic hotel has been largely restored to its former grandeur. 180 rooms. 847-3300.

The Inn Group of hotels includes the **Inn on the Harbor** (359 Thames Street) featuring one-bedroom suites with Pullman kitchens; **Newport Onshore** (405 Thames Street) with one, two and three bedroom suites and the **Inn on Long Wharf**, also with one-bedroom suites. 847-9780.

Large Inns

The **Newport Bay Club** is on the waterfront in a restored 19th-century textile mill listed on the National Register of Historic Places. The Newport Bay Club (America's Cup Avenue and Thames Street) has 36 rooms, all suites or townhouses. 849-8600.

The **Mill Street Inn** is a meticulously-restored 19th-century mill located on Historic Hill. The Mill Street Inn offers elegant townhouses and suites, some with breathtaking views of the harbor. Contemporary furnishings complement a decor of rustic brick and exposed beams. Each of the 23 suites features a queen-size bed and sofa and luxurious fabrics and fixtures. The Inn was recently listed on the National Register of Historic Places. Maid service is twice a day, and tea is served in the afternoon. Parking is provided. 75 Mill Street. 849-9500.

The **Inn at Castle Hill** (Ocean Drive) is a magnificent cedar-shingled mansion, built in 1874 for world traveler, Alexander Agassiz. The elegant interior is filled with antiques, lavishly carved woods (hand-painted wall panels, inlaid woodwork and ornately carved furniture) and Oriental furnishings. Each of the ten rooms in the main house is architecturally and decoratively unique. Located at the entrance to Narragansett Bay, the view can't be beat. No televisions or telephones will disturb your escape. 849-3800.

The **Inntowne** is a restored colonial inn located in the midst of downtown activity (corner of Thames and Mary streets), across from the Brick Marketplace. Breakfast and afternoon tea served in the elegant Tea Room. 26 rooms, phone 846-9200.

The **Cliff Walk Manor**, built in 1855, was once a seaside mansion. The view is magnificent, from the hotel or the adjoining Cliff Walk. It overlooks First Beach. 19 rooms (16 private bath), 82 Memorial Boulevard, phone 847-1300.

The **Harborside Inn** is on Christie's Landing, just off Thames Street. Suites have wet bars and refrigerators. 14 rooms (10 suites), phone 846-6600.

The **Jailhouse Inn** is the former Newport police station. This historic building, dating back to the early 1700s, has been meticulously restored to an elegant inn. You'll enjoy the jailhouse theme and the art deco decor of the 22 large rooms. 13 Marlborough Street. 847-4638.

Inns, Guest Houses and B & Bs

With so many wonderful historic houses restored and converted to small inns, Newport is a treasure trove of fascinating accommodations. The establishments listed below are only a small part of a large selection of memorable places. To sample an exhaustive listing, contact one of Newport's reservation services. These free services screen all establishments for quality and will handle all the booking and billing arrangements for you. **Anna's Victorian Connection** (phone 849-2489) is particularly recommended. Just let the staff at Anna's know your preferences (location, price, style, type of room), and they'll find the closest match possible. **Bed and Breakfast of Rhode Island** (phone 8491298) is another service with a large listing.

The **Pilgrim House** is a ten-room Victorian inn on Historic Hill (123 Spring Street). You'll find antique rooms, lavish continental breakfast, sherry with shortbread and friendly staff. Spectacular view from third-floor deck. Ask innkeeper Mary Rose Weaver to tell you about the house's questionable repute as a former boarding house. Private parking, phone 849-4210.

The **Inn at Old Beach** is strategically located in historic Victorian Newport (19 Old Beach Road) between Newport center and First Beach. Built in 1879 for physician and commodore Stephen Powell (his wife was the great granddaughter of Noah Webster), this Gothic Victorian house has five guest rooms with private baths. Innkeepers Luke and Cindi Murray have uniquely decorated their house in English country style with each room named after a flower. Romance abounds with canopy beds, hand-painted dressers, fireplaces, wicker loveseats, little antique dresses and all sorts of whimsical touches. Stroll in the garden. 849-3479.

The **Stella Maris Inn** is a French Victorian mansion located in the midst of colonial Newport's historic Point section (91 Washington Street). Innkeepers, Dorothy and Ed Madden completely restored Stella Maris in 1990. They have eight guest rooms decorated with antique furniture, all with private baths. Sit on the spacious front porch overlooking Narragansett Bay, or stroll the expansive and beautifully landscaped grounds. Get the gregarious innkeepers to tell you all about the house and its history as a convent and Gilded Age mansion. Private parking, tennis court, phone 849-2862.

Ivy Lodge is a large Queen Anne Victorian located in Newport's mansion section (12 Clay Street), near Bellevue Avenue. You'll walk into a dramatic 33-foot Gothic entry hall paneled in oak and bordered by a three-story staircase with hand-turned spindles and balconies on the upper floors. Choose from eight spacious guest rooms with porcelain-and-brass beds and wicker furniture. Relax in the comfortable antique furniture of the airy living room, or sit on the spacious wrap-around porch. Innkeepers Maggie and Terry Moy serve breakfast buffet style at a 20-foot dining table. It may include bread pudding, baked apples and homemade breads. Renowned Gilded Age architect Stanford White designed this multi-gabled, bay windowed, formerly vine-covered "cottage" in 1886. 849-6865.

The **Brinley Victorian Inn** (23 Brinley Street) is in Victorian Newport, near Catherine Street. The inn consists of two connected buildings: the mansard roofed 1870 main house (10 rooms) and an adjoining seven-room house dating to 1850. The Brinley is a great romantic getaway. You'll bask in the ambiance of period furniture, Victorian wallpapers, satin and lace window treatments, miniature 19th-century oil lamps and fresh flowers. Unpretentious but attentive concierge service. 849-7645.

The Admirals are a group of three Newport inns. The **Admiral Benbow Inn** is a restored 1855 inn located in colonial Newport on Historic Hill (93 Pelham Street). Each of the 15 rooms is beautifully appointed and has a private bath. Brass beds and antiques abound. The **Admiral Farragut Inn** at 31 Clarke Street is a colonial guest house with hand-made four-poster beds, stenciled armoires and English antiques. The **Admiral Fitzroy Inn** is on lower Thames Street in the midst of the bustling waterfront. Built in 1854 and moved here from Spring Street in the 1980s, the building has 18 beautifully restored rooms. 848-8000.

Sanford-Covell Villa Marina is a Victorian gem on Newport's colonial waterfront (72 Washington Street). Architect William Ralph Emerson (cousin of Ralph Waldo Emerson) designed this house (built in 1870). You'll enter an extraordinary foyer rising 35 feet with a grand staircase, projecting balconies and ornately carved woods. Sit on the back porch and enjoy the sunset over the bay and the refreshing sea breeze. 847-0206.

The **Francis Malbone House** (392 Thames Street) is a unique colonial brick mansion built in 1758. Colonel Malbone was a merchant prince heavily involved in shipping and smuggling (evidence indicates an underground tunnel to the water). The main house and the adjoining counting house have been meticulously restored to their former elegance. Located on lower Thames Street, an oasis of luxury in the middle of the bustle. 846-0392.

The **Covell Guest House** at 43 Farewell Street is close to downtown Newport but in a quiet neighborhood. This Colonial/Victorian was built in 1810 and modified (mansard roof) in 1885. Antique rooms, fresh flowers, private parking. 847-8872.

Cliffside Inn is a Victorian "cottage" built in 1880 as a summer getaway for Governor Thomas Swan of Maryland. In 1897, Saint George's School operated here, and later Newport artist Beatrice Turner lived here. This mansard roofed house has ten rooms with private baths and is just a short walk from Cliff Walk (two Seaview Avenue). Floor-to-ceiling windows, Laura Ashley decor, luxurious fabrics and wall coverings and period furniture complete the turn-of-century ambiance. 847-1811.

Wayside is on Bellevue Avenue near The Elms Mansion. This is a turn-of-the-century mini-mansion with large high-ceilinged rooms. Great detail and decor. Six rooms, private bath. 847-0302.

Located on Clarke Street (number 39) in the Historic Hill section, the **Melville House** is a gable roofed Colonial, built in 1750. You'll find eight rooms and parking. 847-0640.

The **Victorian Ladies** (63 Memorial Boulevard) includes an 1890s classic Victorian main house and adjoining carriage house (altogether nine rooms with private baths). Relax in the courtyard or walk to nearby Cliff Walk. 849-9960.

The charm of the **Marshall Slocum House** is surpassed only by the hospitality of its hostess. You'll instantly feel at home in this large Victorian, conveniently located on fashionable Kay Street (number 29). Five rooms, parking, phone 841-5120.

The recently renovated **Mount Vernon Inn** is a 19th century Victorian located at 26 Mount Vernon Street, a few blocks from Touro Synagogue and Washington Square. 846-6314.

William Ralph Emerson designed **Elm Tree Cottage**, an elegant shingle-style mansion built in 1882 for Mary Channing Eustis, daughter of famed Unitarian clergyman William Ellery Channing. The house is located at 336 Gibbs Avenue near First Beach and Cliff Walk. The large English and French country style rooms have Louis XV beds and elegant linens and fabrics. 849-1610.

Ivy Lodge

SIDE TRIPS

Block Island

For a delightful side trip, try Block Island. Unspoiled and isolated, this rugged windswept island will charm you with its extensive and uncrowded beaches, imposing bluffs, flowered hillsides, meandering stone walls, numerous fresh water ponds and Victorian architecture. Tiny Block Island (seven miles long and three miles wide) is located twelve miles off the Rhode Island mainland. Recently the Nature Conservancy declared Block Island one of the "Last Great Places" in the Western Hemisphere. The island provides a safe haven for thousands of migratory birds and is the home of several species of endangered or rare plants and animals.

Block Island is named for Adrian Block, a Dutch explorer, who visited the island in 1614. Presumably, he was the first white man to land on the island--Narragansett Indians were living there when he arrived. White settlers later arrived (in 1661) from Massachusetts, and they farmed the interior. In the late 1800's, Block Island was a luxurious and popular resort. The construction of a jetty (1876) created a protected harbor and allowed tourist ships access to the island. Large resort hotels sprang up along the waterfront.

Around the turn of the century the tourist boom declined. Recent rejuvenation has rekindled this spirit; Block Island is now billed as the "Bermuda of the North". The main street, Water Street (formerly Front Street), reminds you of a western frontier town. There are no modern buildings; it is unchanged from the 19th century. The shoreline is dominated by three impressive Victorian hotels: The Surf (1876), The New Shoreham (1875) and the National (1888). The "National Hotel" sign is a dominant landmark to arriving ferry passengers. The old City Drug Store on Water Street Square is a fascinating specimen of Victorian gingerbread architecture. There are several fine restaurants and shops along Water Street and adjoining Spring Street. Just north of the Water Street area (called Old Harbor) are several sandy beaches within walking (or bicycling) distance.

Mohegan Bluffs on the southeastern shore offers a magnificent view high above the ocean. Nearby sits the Southeast Light, a brick gingerbread lighthouse built in 1873. On the southwestern side, there are more sandy bluffs and secluded beaches with occasional nude bathing. When exploring Block Island beaches, you may come upon a small shipwreck or even watch hangliders leaping from bluffs.

The "Greenway" is a two-mile series of paths connecting Nathan Mott Park (near the airport) to the south shore. The trails winds through dark forests of twisted vines and a great natural ravine filled with rare plants and animals. Clayhead Nature Trails, on the northeast side, offer a great walk amidst rolling hills, fresh water ponds and secluded beaches.

The Block Island Historical Cemetery is high on a hill near the middle of the island. This lovely site contains the gravestones of 17th and 18th century pioneers. Read the tombstones, they have fascinating tales to tell.

The Great Salt Pond is a large protected cove (called New Harbor) lying in the north central section of the island. This is a popular mooring for sailboats of all kinds. Sandy Point on the northern tip is the breeding ground for the local seagull population. You'll also find the North Light. This historic lighthouse was built in 1867 with Connecticut granite and is being restored as a maritime museum.

Block Island is a peaceful and unhurried escape, and you can make the round-trip in one day. The ferry ride--itself an interesting experience--takes about one and three-quarter hours. The boat leaves Newport from Fort Adams.

Bay Islands Park

Nine locations, scattered throughout Narragansett Bay, make up Bay Islands Park. The park covers 2,300 acres and consists of Prudence, Patience and Hope Islands on the north and Dutch Island, Beavertail, Fort Wetherill, Fort Adams and Brenton Point on the south.

Although surrounded by a busy mainland, most sections of Bay Islands Park are relatively isolated. They offer a variety of views into the pristine beauty of Narragansett Bay, such as the placid seclusion of Prudence Island or the surf pounding on the rugged coastline of Beavertail.

Prudence Island, located at the center of Narragansett Bay, contains 1,300 acres of park land. The park is on the southern and northern end of the island; the middle is privately-owned. South Prudence has a rocky coastline and is covered with forests and marshes. Hiking, camping and naturalist programs are available.

Prudence Island is accessible by ferry from Bristol. A day trip will take you to a time warp of quaint cottages and dilapidated cars. There's no auto registration requirement, and everyone shuttles around in classic clunkers. Prudence Island also has a winery, a restaurant and some rustic stores.

North Prudence is designated a National Estuarine Sanctuary and is protected from development. Visitors can hike along ten miles of trails winding through forest, marshes, scrub brush, wind-blown hills, and sheltered inlets. Patience Island adjoins Prudence and is part of the same protected area.

Hope Island consists of 92 acres and is a nesting area for over 2,000 northeast wading birds (ibis, egrets and herons). The bird colony is protected from disturbance; visitors are not permitted during the nesting period (April to July).

Dutch Island, just west of Jamestown (Conanicut Island), was the site of a 19th-century fort protecting the West Passage to Narragansett Bay. Ruins are still visible. 17th-century Dutch traders moored in the protected harbor.

Fort Wetherill's craggy cliffs of granite (a sea bird nesting area) guard the southern coast of Conanicut Island from the waves of Rhode Island Sound. You can picnic on the cliffs and view the magnificent sailing vessels plying the East Passage.

Beavertail, a southern peninsula of Conanicut Island, offers breathtaking views of the crashing, spraying Atlantic; the tip of the beaver's tail thrusts southward slicing the pounding surf. The 186-acre park includes bicycle paths and a shoreline trail along the coves and beaches. A 19th-century (1854) lighthouse still operates and contains a visitor center. Fort Adams and Brenton Point are described elsewhere in this book.

Many of the locations in Bay Islands Park can be explored by guided tours led by naturalists. The island locations can be visited by private boat or scheduled ferry service. For further information contact the Rhode Island Department of Environmental Management.

Green Animals

Green Animals (Route 114 at Cory Lane, Portsmouth) is the name given to the topiary gardens at the former Brayton estate. The gardens contain about 80 sculptured trees and shrubs, rose gardens, trained fruit trees (growing flat against a wall) and several other gardens and trees. The most spectacular of all are the huge sculptured green animals; some are twenty-six feet high. All are exquisitely sculptured from privet hedges originally planted by Thomas Brayton. The hedges grew for twenty years before reaching their full size and form. The meticulously groomed animals include a giraffe, elephant, lion, dog, cat, donkey, boar and peacock--there's also a policeman and a sailboat. These are all beautifully arranged in the midst of a formal garden. Green Animals is owned by the Preservation Society of Newport County.

Prescott Farm

Prescott Farm (West Main Road, Middletown) is a re-creation of a colonial Rhode Island farm. It includes a museum with colonial furniture, an ancient working windmill and a country store stocked with items typical of the time. You can buy stone-ground cornmeal, ground by the windmill's three-ton granite stones.

Henry Overing's country estate (Overing House, c. 1730) is also at Prescott Farm. This house was the country rendezvous where a band of daring patriots captured the hated General Prescott, commander of the occupying British army. In July of 1777 a small American force, led by Colonel William Barton, dragged General Prescott screaming in his nightshirt from the bed of his mistress, Mrs. Overing.

Prescott Farm is run by the Newport Restoration Foundation and is open to the public.

Whitehall

George Berkeley, the eminent Anglican churchman, built Whitehall (Berkeley Avenue, Middletown) in 1729. Berkeley spent three years in Newport before returning to England. During this time, he wrote important theological treatises and was a key part of the Newport cultural climate--he helped start Redwood Library.

This colonial red country house is large but not ostentatious. Whitehall has been restored by the Society of Colonial Dames and is open to the public.

Newport Naval Facility

Situated north of Newport Bridge on Coasters Harbor Island and Coddington Point, the Newport Naval Facility is the home of the Naval War College, the Naval Education and Training Center and the Naval Undersea Warfare Center.

Newport has a rich naval tradition; the Naval Academy temporarily moved here during the Civil War. In 1869, a torpedo station was built on Goat Island; the War College was established in 1884.

The Naval War College is the oldest (1884) naval war college in the world and the highest educational institution in the navy. It is considered the premier educational facility for naval tactics and strategy; senior officers from all over the world attend courses. The Naval War College Museum has all sorts of exhibits depicting the history of the navy in Narragansett Bay as well as the history of naval warfare as studied at the Naval War College. The museum is open to the public. Enter the base at Gate One near the Naval Hospital.

TIPS

Newport Life

Obviously Newport is not Disneyworld, it's a vibrant community with a rich cultural heritage and a diverse population. While tourism is an important part of the economy, there's also a large Navy presence, significant marine and fishing industries, lots of high-tech research and development and an important university. So, as you might expect, not everyone loves tourists, but most Newporters are hospitable and welcome visitors graciously. However, two things are particularly irksome (and worrisome) to local residents: late-night noise (people have to get up for work in the morning) and the threat of deterioration in the quality of life, where boutiques and condominiums replace neighborhood stores and houses.
Reminder: Thames Street is pronounced with a long "a" (rhymes with flames), not like the English version.

Off Season

Visit Newport in the late fall, winter or early spring, and you'll be pleasantly surprised. The crowds are greatly diminished, and most of the restaurant, shops and points of interest are open. The fall is particularly recommended, the weather is usually great, with crisp clear days and beautiful sunsets. You can leisurely take historic walking tours, park on the street and generally enjoy the relaxed pace.

Getting Around

Downtown Newport presents a logistical challenge to the tourist; getting around can be difficult. The problems are driving and parking. Try not to do too much of either, they can be hazardous to your health. Newport streets are usually narrow, frequently one-way and almost always crowded. If you're not careful, you'll be on a merry-go-round looking for a place to get off. Parking lots are in short supply, and towing is common. So walk or ride a bicycle if possible.

Gateway Center

This is definitely the place to go before touring Newport. It's Newport's resource and information headquarters, where you can view a spectacular 16-screen audio/video show on Newport, buy tour tickets, reserve a room, buy books, pick up all sorts of free brochures and maps, park your car (half-hour free), pick up a tour bus, visit the restroom, and ask the friendly and knowledgeable staff just about any question on Newport. The Gateway Center is located on America's Cup Avenue, next to the Newport Marriott Hotel. The Newport County Convention and Visitors Bureau operates the Gateway Center. It's open every day, for more information call 849-8098.

Other Things To Do

Visiting mansions, taking walking tours and eating in restaurants aren't the only things to do in Newport. There's so much to do, try some of these.

Take a guided walking tour -You'll find expert guidance on walking tours of colonial Newport. Newport on Foot offers a 90 minute tour leaving twice a day from the Gateway Center (check for posted departure times). The tour focuses on the architectural and cultural evolution of Newport. The Newport Historical Society conducts tours of the colonial center of Newport, covering Touro Synagogue, Colony House, Brick Market and Trinity Church and a variety of historic houses. The tours, given on Fridays and Saturdays at 10 a.m., include architecture as well as the history of houses and their occupants. Phone 846-0813.

Go to the beach - Newport has several fine beaches. Probably the most popular is First Beach (Easton's Beach). Located at the foot of Memorial Boulevard near the Middletown line, this half-mile strand has bath houses, concessions, parking and life guards. The waves are good and high. Around Ocean Drive, you'll find Reject Beach (no services), a nicknamed public strip adjoining private and exclusive Bailey's Beach. Continue around Ocean Drive, and you'll soon find Gooseberry Beach in a lovely protected cove. Gooseberry also has bath houses and life guards. Private Hazards Beach is in the same cove. Fort Adams State Park has a small beach with lots of things to do and a great view of the city. Small and calm, King Park Beach (no services) is along Wellington Avenue on Newport harbor.
Middletown has two great beaches. Second Beach (Sachuest Beach) is nearly two miles long with full services and good surf. Nearby Third Beach is on the relatively calm Sakonnet River and is a good place to sail or wind surf. Sachuest Point National Wildlife Refuge is between these beaches. You can walk the many trails and enjoy the seaside environment.

Take a harbor cruise - Oldport Marine Services offers several tours daily, departing from Sayer's Wharf (near the Newport Yachting Center on America's Cup Avenue). The 55-foot tour boat, (Amazing Grace) holds 100 passengers. Phone 849-2111. The Viking Queen (140 passengers) and the Viking Princess (49 passengers) sail several times daily from the Goat Island marina. Call 847-6921.

Go shopping -Shops are all over Newport, particularly along Thames Street and America's Cup Avenue. The <u>Brick Marketplace</u>, between Thames Street and America's Cup Avenue, <u>Bannister's and Bowen's Wharf</u>, upper <u>Bellevue Avenue</u>, upper <u>Spring Street</u> and lower <u>Thames Street</u> are the most popular. Also there are lots of antique shops along <u>Franklin Street</u>.

Go fly a kite - <u>Brenton Point State Park</u> on Ocean Drive is an ideal place for kite flying, sea breezes and open spaces provide perfect conditions. On a good day, you'll see all manner of odd-shaped and spectacular flying devices zooming around.

Go to a dinner theater - Ride out to Connell Highway, near the Admiral Kalbfus rotary and spend a delightful evening at the <u>Newport Playhouse and Cabaret Restaurant</u>. This is one of the best deals in Newport or anywhere else. It's an intimate playhouse, but it's also a fine buffet restaurant. It works like this. You're party arrives at a private table in the restaurant to enjoy a sumptuous and generous buffet dinner consisting of roast beef, fresh fish, roasted chicken, beef and peppers, Italian sausages, fresh ham and beans, oven-roasted potatoes, all sorts of vegetables, three kinds of salads and fresh-baked desserts. You'll need to select a platter instead of a regular dinner plate to accommodate this vast array of food. After dinner, you're ushered into the intimate 140-seat theatre to enjoy a first-rate play (often a comedy). After the show, its back to your table for a rousing and highly creative cabaret. Many enjoy the cabaret even more than the play.
Don't be surprised when you see your waitperson acting in the play or singing in the cabaret. The waitstaff, cooks, bartenders, and even the host are all actors and singers. The restaurant is decorated in theatre motif with framed pictures of actors, actresses and historic playbills on the walls.
The price for everything excepts drinks is $29.95, and there's no tipping on dinner (only on cocktails). The well-poured cocktails are the best in Newport. You'll agree that producer Matt Siravo and manager Jonathan Perry have put together a quality and fun-filled experience. There's lots of parking. Phone 848-7529.

Ride a dinner train -The <u>Newport Star Clipper Dinner Train</u> offers luxurious dining aboard vintage dinner cars restored to their former elegance. You'll enjoy a four-course meal (prepared on-board) while you travel along the eastern shore of Narragansett Bay passing, deep gullies, rocky coves, boatyards and marshes. The three-hour (7 p.m. to 10 p.m.) scenic journey begins and ends at the railroad depot on America's Cup Avenue near the Gateway Center. Special entertainment evenings feature murder mysteries or Jazz. Phone 849-7550.

Newport, Touring Sections

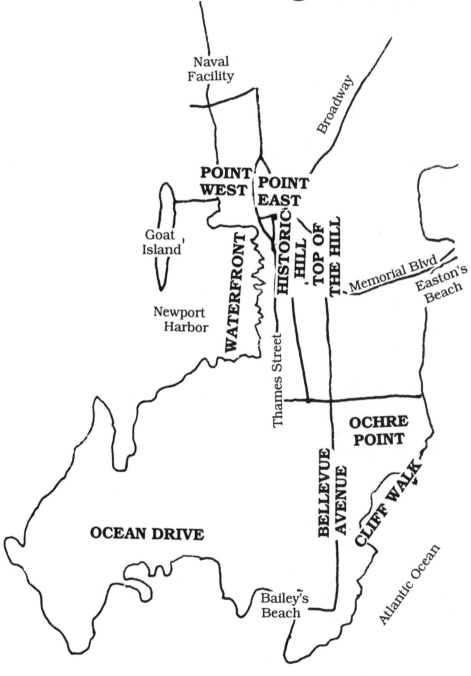

Naval
Facility

Broadway

POINT
WEST

POINT
EAST

Goat
Island

WATERFRONT

HISTORIC HILL

TOP OF THE HILL

Memorial Blvd

Easton's
Beach

Newport
Harbor

Thames Street

OCHRE
POINT

BELLEVUE
AVENUE

CLIFF WALK

OCEAN DRIVE

Bailey's
Beach

Atlantic Ocean